TEST YOUR CARD PLAY

Other Books by Hugh Kelsey
published by Houghton Mifflin Company

Instant Guide to Bridge
Hugh Kelsey and Ron Klinger

TEST YOUR
CARD PLAY

VOLUMES 1 & 2

Hugh Kelsey

A Master Bridge Series title
in conjunction with Peter Crawley

Houghton Mifflin Company
Boston   New York
1993

For information about permission to reproduce selections
from this book, write to Permissions, Houghton Mifflin Company,
215 Park Avenue South, New York, New York 10003.

Library of Congress Cataloguing-in-Publication Data
Kelsey, H. W. (Hugh Walter)
Test your card play / Hugh Kelsey.
v. <1-2; in 1 >
Originally published : London : V. Gollancz in association with
P. Crawley, 1990– .
"A Master bridge series title in conjunction with Peter Crawley."
ISBN 0-395-65665-6
1. Contract bridge — Miscellanea.
I. Title. II. Series: Master bridge series.
GV1282.32.K359 1993
795.41'53 — dc20   92-35311
CIP

Printed in the United States of America
BP 10 9 8 7 6 5 4 3 2 1

TEST YOUR CARD PLAY
VOLUME 1

INTRODUCTION

This little volume marks the start of a new series of quiz-books designed to test your dummy play and defence. Not all of the problems are original. Some have been taken from *Test Your Match Play*, *The Tough Game* and *The Needle Match* books which are now out of print. A new generation of readers will not have seen these hands, and in any case there are enough fresh problems here to whet the most jaded appetite.

The problems are set on odd-numbered pages with only two hands on view. A bidding sequence is supplied in every case, but the bidding is important only in so far as it provides a clue to the nature of the opponents' holdings. The opening lead is specified, and in some cases the play to the first few tricks is given. At this point you are invited to take over. Try to work out the best line of play or defence for yourself before reading on. In case of difficulty, you may find some inspiration in the next paragraph where the options are reviewed and the issues clarified. The solution and the complete deal are given overleaf.

The hands have been arranged in no particular order except that they have been roughly graded according to difficulty, the easier ones coming in the early part of the book. You can regard your card play as satisfactory if you come up with the right answer to twenty or more of these problems. Twenty-five correct is an excellent score, thirty is magnificent and thirty-five unbelievable. Good luck!

PROBLEM 1

♠ 8 6
♡ A 6
♢ A J 10
♣ A K 8 6 5 3

♠ A Q J 7
♡ K 8 7
♢ K Q 5 4
♣ 10 2

Love all.
Dealer South.

The Bidding

SOUTH	WEST	NORTH	EAST
1 ♠	Pass	2 ♣	Pass
2 NT	Pass	6 NT	Pass
Pass	Pass		

The Lead

West leads the nine of diamonds to dummy's ten. How do you plan the play?

Review

Nine top tricks are in view, and the club suit is the most likely source of extra tricks. What is the best way to tackle the suit?

Solution

A normal 3–2 club break will see you home. Failing that, you will need the spade finesse and a squeeze. There is a temptation to play a small club from dummy at trick two, but that would not be a bright idea. If East wins and returns a spade you will have to make a premature commitment before you know if the clubs are breaking. The correct move is to cash one top club and continue with a low club. Whatever happens you will know what you need from the spade suit.

The complete deal:

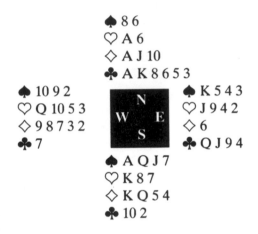

♠ 8 6
♡ A 6
♢ A J 10
♣ A K 8 6 5 3

♠ 10 9 2
♡ Q 10 5 3
♢ 9 8 7 3 2
♣ 7

♠ K 5 4 3
♡ J 9 4 2
♢ 6
♣ Q J 9 4

♠ A Q J 7
♡ K 8 7
♢ K Q 5 4
♣ 10 2

In practice East wins the second club and West shows out. East returns a heart, and you must be careful to win in hand with the king. After a diamond to the ace, you finesse successfully in spades and cash the remaining diamonds. East can discard hearts on the diamonds, but when you play a heart to the ace he is squeezed in the black suits and twelve tricks roll in.

PROBLEM 2

♠ A J 10 6
♡ A Q J 8 7 4
♢ A 7
♣ 6

```
    N
 W    E
    S
```

♠ K Q 9 5 3
♡ 6 3
♢ 9 6 3
♣ A Q 8

N–S game.
Dealer North.

The Bidding

WEST	NORTH	EAST	SOUTH
	1 ♡	Pass	1 ♠
Pass	3 ♢	Pass	4 ♣
Pass	4 ♠	Pass	4 NT
Pass	5 ♠	Pass	5 NT
Pass	6 ♣	Pass	6 ♠
Pass	Pass	Pass	

The Lead

West leads the king of diamonds to dummy's ace. You draw the outstanding trumps with the ace and king. How should you continue?

Review

The diamond lead has attacked the weak spot and you are forced to rely on some lucky finessing. How should you tackle the hand?

Solution

This is just a matter of marshalling the odds to give yourself the best possible chance. There are two ways of trying for the slam. A successful heart finesse would mean that you could afford a diamond loser, although in practice you would make all thirteen tricks by setting up the hearts and discarding both losing diamonds from your hand.

The alternative is to take the club finesse, hoping to discard dummy's diamond on the ace of clubs. If this goes well you can afford to lose a heart trick.

The probability of success is the same for each finesse, but the club finesse is the better shot because it allows you the additional chance of trying to drop a singleton king of hearts in the East hand. You should therefore play a heart to the ace at trick four. If nothing exciting happens, continue with a club for a finesse of the queen.

The complete deal:

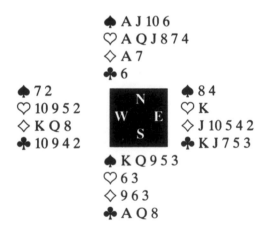

```
                ♠ A J 10 6
                ♡ A Q J 8 7 4
                ◇ A 7
                ♣ 6
    ♠ 7 2                      ♠ 8 4
    ♡ 10 9 5 2       N         ♡ K
    ◇ K Q 8      W     E       ◇ J 10 5 4 2
    ♣ 10 9 4 2       S         ♣ K J 7 5 3
                ♠ K Q 9 5 3
                ♡ 6 3
                ◇ 9 6 3
                ♣ A Q 8
```

As it happens, the fall of the heart king solves all your problems.

PROBLEM 3

♠ K 4
♡ Q 8 7 3
◇ A 8 6 4
♣ Q 5 2

♠ Q 10 9 7 6 3 2
♡ K 5
◇ 3
♣ A K 7

Game all.
Dealer North.

The Bidding

WEST	NORTH	EAST	SOUTH
	Pass	Pass	1 ♠
2 ♡	Dble	3 ◇	3 ♠
Pass	4 ♠	Pass	Pass
Pass			

The Lead

West starts with the ace and another heart, and East ruffs the second round with the five of spades. The king of diamonds is returned to dummy's ace. How should you proceed?

Review

In spite of suffering a heart ruff you are still a heavy favourite to make the contract. All you have to do is avoid the loss of two further trump tricks.

Solution

The bidding marks the ace of spades in the West hand, and a lead of the king of spades at this point will be fatal if West has all the remaining trumps.

How can you find out if this is the position? Quite simply, by leading the queen of hearts from dummy at trick four. East is bound to ruff if he can find another trump in his hand, since for all he knows you may be planning to discard a losing diamond on the queen of hearts. If East fails to ruff, it is reasonable to place the remaining trumps with West.

The complete deal:

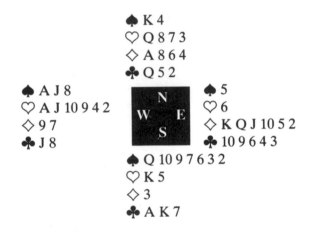

♠ K 4
♡ Q 8 7 3
◇ A 8 6 4
♣ Q 5 2

♠ A J 8
♡ A J 10 9 4 2
◇ 9 7
♣ J 8

♠ 5
♡ 6
◇ K Q J 10 5 2
♣ 10 9 6 4 3

♠ Q 10 9 7 6 3 2
♡ K 5
◇ 3
♣ A K 7

When East discards on the queen of hearts, you ruff it yourself and run the ten of spades through West to trap his jack.

PROBLEM 4

♠ K Q J 6 5
♡ 8 4
◇ A K Q 4
♣ Q 6

```
    N
W       E
    S
```

♠ A 8 7
♡ A K 9 5

Love all.
Dealer East.

◇ 8 7 3 2
♣ A 9

The Bidding

WEST	NORTH	EAST	SOUTH
		Pass	1 ♡
Dble	2 ♡	3 ♣	Pass
Pass	Pass		

The Lead

On your lead of the ace of hearts North plays the queen. How do you continue?

Review

You can see four tricks for the defence in your own hand. Where might a fifth be found?

Solution

You can hardly expect partner to contribute a trump trick, and the chances of a diamond ruff are nebulous, to say the least.

That leaves only the heart suit, and there is no reason why you should not enjoy a third heart trick once dummy's trumps have been removed. It will not do to release the ace of trumps too early, of course, for declarer may be able to take discards on the diamonds when trumps have been drawn.

The right move is to switch to the nine of clubs at trick two. Your plan is to win the second round of trumps, scoring one club, three hearts and one spade to put the contract one down.

The complete deal:

♠ 10 9 4 2
♡ Q J 10 3
◇ 9 5
♣ 7 4 3

♠ K Q J 6 5
♡ 8 4
◇ A K Q 4
♣ Q 6

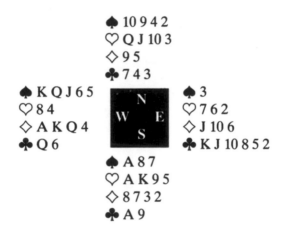

♠ 3
♡ 7 6 2
◇ J 10 6
♣ K J 10 8 5 2

♠ A 8 7
♡ A K 9 5
◇ 8 7 3 2
♣ A 9

PROBLEM 5

♠ K Q 5
♡ 9 6 3
♢ Q J 7 3
♣ Q 6 5

♠ A 7 2
♡ A 8 7
♢ K 6 2
♣ A 8 4 3

Love all.
Dealer North.

The Bidding

WEST	NORTH	EAST	SOUTH
	Pass	Pass	1 NT
Pass	3 NT	Pass	Pass
Pass			

The Lead

West leads the seven of clubs. How do you plan the play?

Review

With only five tricks on top, you need to develop a second club trick and to establish three winners in diamonds. What is the best way to set about it?

Solution

If the seven of clubs is a normal fourth-highest lead, East is marked with just one higher card in the suit. This can hardly be the king, for with J 10 9 7 West would have led the jack. It must therefore be perfectly safe to go up with the queen of clubs at trick one.

There remains the matter of tackling the diamonds. It makes no difference how you play if the diamonds are 3–3, but correct technique will also win three tricks when West has a doubleton ace. Enter hand with the ace of spades and lead a low diamond to dummy's jack. If it wins, return to the ace of clubs (not the ace of . hearts which might release too many winners for the defence) and lead another low diamond. If the ace pops up or if the suit breaks 3–3, you have your nine tricks.

The complete deal:

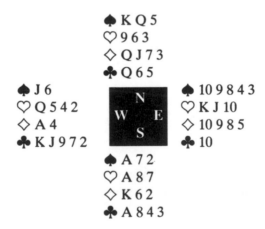

```
              ♠ K Q 5
              ♡ 9 6 3
              ◇ Q J 7 3
              ♣ Q 6 5
♠ J 6                        ♠ 10 9 8 4 3
♡ Q 5 4 2          N         ♡ K J 10
◇ A 4          W       E     ◇ 10 9 8 5
♣ K J 9 7 2        S         ♣ 10
              ♠ A 7 2
              ♡ A 8 7
              ◇ K 6 2
              ♣ A 8 4 3
```

Note that it is not good enough to play low from dummy at trick one, relying on making the queen of clubs later. That puts you a tempo behind and a heart switch holds you to eight tricks.

PROBLEM 6

♠ Q J 5 2
♡ J 4
♢ 8 6 5 3
♣ K 10 3

♠ A 6
♡ A K 9 8 7 5 2
♢ 7
♣ Q 9 5

E–W game.
Dealer North.

The Bidding

WEST	NORTH	EAST	SOUTH
	Pass	Pass	4 ♡
Pass	Pass	Pass	

The Lead

On the lead of the ace of diamonds East drops the queen. West continues with the two of diamonds to his partner's ten. You ruff and draw trumps in two rounds, West showing up with the queen. What do you do now?

Review

All you have to do is avoid the loss of three tricks in the black suits. How can you make the most of your chances?

Solution

Your tenth trick may come from a successful finesse in either clubs or spades. It may not be easy to find an entry for the spade finesse, however, especially if East has both of the missing club honours.

If you are to avail yourself of all the chances in the black suits there is only one way to tackle the clubs. At trick five you should lead the nine of clubs and run it when West plays low. If the nine wins the trick or draws the ace, you have your tenth trick immediately. If the nine loses to the jack, you can make sure of an entry for the spade finesse by overtaking the queen of clubs with the king on the second round.

The complete deal:

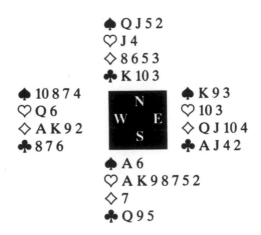

```
                    ♠ Q J 5 2
                    ♡ J 4
                    ◇ 8 6 5 3
                    ♣ K 10 3
   ♠ 10 8 7 4            N            ♠ K 9 3
   ♡ Q 6                              ♡ 10 3
   ◇ A K 9 2       W         E        ◇ Q J 10 4
   ♣ 8 7 6                            ♣ A J 4 2
                       S
                    ♠ A 6
                    ♡ A K 9 8 7 5 2
                    ◇ 7
                    ♣ Q 9 5
```

PROBLEM 7

♠ 9 6 5 2
♡ 10 9 6 3
♢ A K J 6
♣ 10

♠ A 10 3
♡ K Q 8 7 2
♢ Q 5
♣ A Q 5

Game all.
Dealer South.

The Bidding

SOUTH	WEST	NORTH	EAST
1 ♡	Pass	4 ♡	Pass
Pass	Pass		

The Lead

West leads the four of spades and East plays the king. How do you plan the play?

Review

This is a fine contract. If you can get both spade losers away on the diamonds you should make eleven tricks, losing only two trumps. Are there any dangers?

Solution

The risk is that West may have a doubleton diamond. Then, if you try to get both spade losers away, you may end up losing a spade and *three* trump tricks.

It does not pay to be greedy at this game. The safe play is to hold up the ace of spades, win the second round and *then* play three rounds of diamonds, discarding your remaining spade. If West ruffs, it is likely that you will lose no more than one further trick in trumps.

The complete deal:

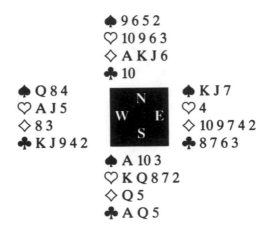

You see what will happen to anyone who wins the first trick and plays on diamonds? West ruffs, plays the eight of spades to his partner's jack, and makes two further trump tricks on the diamond return.

PROBLEM 8

♠ A J 6 2
♡ J 4 2
◇ 9 5
♣ K J 7 4

♠ 7
♡ A K Q 10 8 5

Love all.　　◇ Q J 3

Dealer South.　♣ 10 6 2

The Bidding

SOUTH	WEST	NORTH	EAST
1 ♡	Pass	Pass	2 ♠
Pass	4 ♠	Pass	Pass
Pass			

The Lead

On your lead of the ace of hearts North plays the nine and East the six. How do you continue?

Review

It looks as though the missing hearts are divided 2–2 in the unseen hands. You still need two tricks outside the heart suit to defeat the contract, and the prospects are far from rosy. What do you need to find in partner's hand?

Solution

Partner cannot have much since he passed your opening bid, but there is just room for him to have a king and a queen. You must hope that he has the king of diamonds and the queen of clubs. Does this mean that you should cash the king of hearts and switch to diamonds?

The trouble with this is that it may help declarer to bring off an end-play. You need East to have three clubs along with his probable six spades and two hearts. That leaves him with only two diamonds, and after winning the diamond switch he would play a spade to the ace, ruff the jack of hearts, draw the last trump, and exit in diamonds to enforce a club return which could be fatal from either side of the table.

To protect yourself against this threat you must switch to the queen of diamonds at trick two

The complete deal:

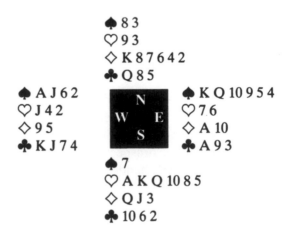

```
                  ♠ 8 3
                  ♡ 9 3
                  ◇ K 8 7 6 4 2
                  ♣ Q 8 5
   ♠ A J 6 2                    ♠ K Q 10 9 5 4
   ♡ J 4 2            N         ♡ 7 6
   ◇ 9 5         W       E      ◇ A 10
   ♣ K J 7 4          S         ♣ A 9 3
                  ♠ 7
                  ♡ A K Q 10 8 5
                  ◇ Q J 3
                  ♣ 10 6 2
```

After the diamond switch at trick two declarer has no chance of an end-play and has to fall back on the losing club finesse.

PROBLEM 9

♠ Q 6 5
♡ 9 8 5 3
♢ A 8 4
♣ A 6 2

♠ A J 10
♡ A J 6
♢ K 7 2
♣ Q 9 5 4

Game all.
Dealer South.

The Bidding

SOUTH	WEST	NORTH	EAST
1 NT	Pass	3 NT	Pass
Pass	Pass		

The Lead

West leads the king of hearts on which East plays the two. You win with the ace and return the jack of hearts. West takes his queen and ten and continues with a fourth heart, East discarding a spade, a diamond and a club. You throw a diamond on the fourth heart and lead the queen of spades to the king and ace. What now?

Review

You need two tricks from the clubs and, since East appears to have started with a 4–1–4–4 distribution, it should be possible to make them. All you have to do is guess the location of the king of clubs. How do you proceed?

Solution

Probabilities indicate that East is twice as likely to have the club king as West, but the fact that West continued hearts suggests that he has a potential entry somewhere. It would be a pity to have your queen gobbled up by the doubleton king on the second round.

Are there any extra chances? Well, you can afford to lose two clubs provided that West is kept off lead. The way to cater for the king and a small card in the West hand is to lead the nine of clubs and run it if West plays low. Then you can play the ace on the second round and continue with a third club which only East can win. If West plays the jack or ten of clubs on your nine, you will have to win with the ace and hope to guess well on the second round.

The complete deal:

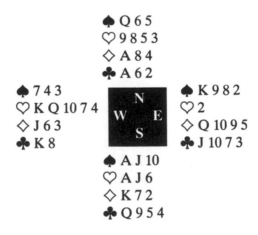

```
               ♠ Q 6 5
               ♡ 9 8 5 3
               ◇ A 8 4
               ♣ A 6 2
  ♠ 7 4 3                      ♠ K 9 8 2
  ♡ K Q 10 7 4      N          ♡ 2
  ◇ J 6 3       W       E      ◇ Q 10 9 5
  ♣ K 8             S          ♣ J 10 7 3
               ♠ A J 10
               ♡ A J 6
               ◇ K 7 2
               ♣ Q 9 5 4
```

As it happens, the play of the nine of clubs brings in ten tricks without difficulty.

PROBLEM 10

♠ A Q 5
♥ J 3
♦ A 9 5
♣ A 10 8 6 2

♠ J 10 4
♥ A K Q 10 9 6 2
♦ –
♣ 9 5 3

Love all.
Dealer North.

The Bidding

WEST	NORTH	EAST	SOUTH
	1 ♣	Pass	2 ♥
Pass	2 NT	Pass	4 ♥
Pass	6 ♥	Pass	Pass
Pass			

The Lead

West leads the six of diamonds against your slam. How do you plan the play?

Review

This is a reasonable contract and you will have no difficulty in taking twelve tricks if the spade finesse is right. Are there any extra chances?

Solution

Having escaped a spade lead, you can avoid the hazard of the finesse whenever the clubs break 3–2. The key move is to play the nine of diamonds from dummy at trick one and discard a club from your hand. The idea is to give up an early trick to East, who cannot profitably attack spades from his side of the table.

You win a trump return in hand, play a club to the ace, discard your last club on the ace of diamonds and ruff a club high. If the suit breaks favourably you can return to the table with the jack of hearts and ruff another club high. After drawing trumps you will be in a position to discard your spade losers on the established clubs.

The complete deal:

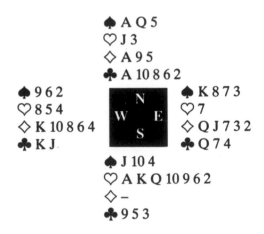

```
                ♠ A Q 5
                ♡ J 3
                ◇ A 9 5
                ♣ A 10 8 6 2
  ♠ 9 6 2          N        ♠ K 8 7 3
  ♡ 8 5 4                   ♡ 7
  ◇ K 10 8 6 4   W    E     ◇ Q J 7 3 2
  ♣ K J              S      ♣ Q 7 4
                ♠ J 10 4
                ♡ A K Q 10 9 6 2
                ◇ –
                ♣ 9 5 3
```

Note that the recommended play carries very little risk. If the clubs prove to be 4–1 you can always fall back on the spade finesse.

PROBLEM 11

♠ A 7 6 3
♡ 10 8 5 2
♢ K 8 3
♣ K 2

♠ 5 4
♡ A Q 7 6 4
♢ A J 6
♣ Q 8 4

Love all.
Dealer South.

The Bidding

SOUTH	WEST	NORTH	EAST
1 ♡	Pass	3 ♡	Pass
4 ♡	Pass	Pass	Pass

The Lead

West leads the queen of spades. How do you plan the play?

Review

The situation is far from comfortable. You have a sure loser in each of the black suits, a potential loser in diamonds and a shaky trump holding. Is there a case for safety-playing the trumps by cashing the ace on the first round?

Solution

At the moment you do not know if you can afford a trump loser, but you can find out by testing the diamonds. Win the first trick with the ace of spades and play a low diamond for a finesse of the jack. If this loses to the queen, you will need to find East with king and another heart.

If the diamond finesse succeeds you can afford to lose a trump trick, and you can guard against losing two by cashing the heart ace at trick three.

The complete deal:

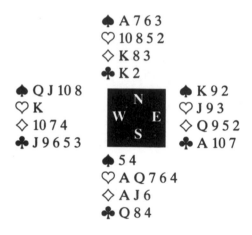

♠ A 7 6 3
♥ 10 8 5 2
♦ K 8 3
♣ K 2

♠ Q J 10 8
♥ K
♦ 10 7 4
♣ J 9 6 5 3

♠ K 9 2
♥ J 9 3
♦ Q 9 5 2
♣ A 10 7

♠ 5 4
♥ A Q 7 6 4
♦ A J 6
♣ Q 8 4

It often helps to retain control if you concede the first trick in a suit to the opponents, but it would not be a good idea on this hand. If you play low from dummy at trick one, East may overtake with the king and switch to the three of hearts, forcing you to commit yourself in trumps before you know if the diamond finesse is working.

PROBLEM 12

♠ Q 5
♡ Q 7 2
♢ Q 10 7 6 3
♣ 8 6 4

```
        N
    W       E
        S
```

♠ K J
♡ A J 6 3
♢ A J 2
♣ A Q 9 5

N–S game.
Dealer South.

The Bidding

SOUTH	WEST	NORTH	EAST
2 NT	Pass	3 ♡	3 ♠
4 ♡	4 ♠	Dble	Pass
Pass	Pass		

The Lead

Your ace of hearts wins the first trick, but East ruffs the next heart and leads a spade. You win with the king and North follows with the four. East ruffs the heart return and plays another spade to the queen, North completing an echo with the three. Next comes the three of diamonds on which North plays the eight and East the king. How do you plan the defence?

Review

It is annoying when the opponents insist on sacrificing against your big hands, and it can be even more annoying if you fail to exact the maximum penalty. How do you go for the jugular?

Solution

The cards played by partner mark him with a third trump and a doubleton diamond, and it should be clear that you can engineer a ruff for him by winning at once with the ace of diamonds and returning the diamond jack to dummy's queen. The declarer is thus locked on the table with no way of drawing the outstanding trump. You can win a club lead, give partner his diamond ruff, and subsequently score one or two further tricks in clubs.

The complete deal:

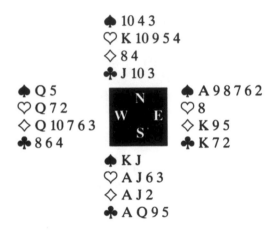

```
                    ♠ 10 4 3
                    ♡ K 10 9 5 4
                    ◇ 8 4
                    ♣ J 10 3
  ♠ Q 5                              ♠ A 9 8 7 6 2
  ♡ Q 7 2           N                ♡ 8
  ◇ Q 10 7 6 3    W   E              ◇ K 9 5
  ♣ 8 6 4           S                ♣ K 7 2
                    ♠ K J
                    ♡ A J 6 3
                    ◇ A J 2
                    ♣ A Q 9 5
```

As you can see, you need the diamond ruff to achieve a satisfactory penalty of 800.

PROBLEM 13

♠ K 5
♡ A 7 3
◇ K 8 7 2
♣ A K 5 4

♠ A Q J 10 7 2
♡ 6
◇ 6 5 4 3
♣ 7 6

N–S game.
Dealer East.

The Bidding

WEST	NORTH	EAST	SOUTH
		1 ♡	1 ♠
4 ♡	4 ♠	Pass	Pass
Pass			

The Lead

West leads the five of hearts to dummy's ace. How do you plan the play?

Review

This looks like a good contract. You can count nine top tricks and there are excellent chances of a tenth trick in diamonds. Although the diamond ace is sure to be wrong, a 3–2 split will see you home. Are there any snags to look out for?

Solution

On the bidding you are quite likely to run into a bad trump break. If you draw trumps immediately and a defender shows out on the second round, you will not have time to set up your diamond trick. Four rounds of trumps will leave you with only two – not enough to withstand the heart force that will come each time the defenders gain the lead.

You need to find the diamonds 3–2 but there is no need to rely on a 3–2 trump break as well. The way to protect yourself is to set up the diamond trick before touching trumps. Lead a small diamond from the table at trick two. You can ruff the heart return and duck a diamond, ruff the next heart and play a third diamond. If the defenders play a fourth heart at this point you can discard your remaining diamond and ruff in dummy. On any other return you will be able to draw trumps and score your established diamond.

The complete deal:

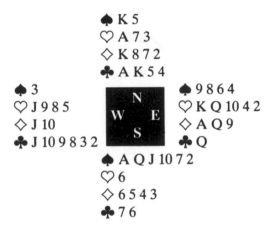

```
                  ♠ K 5
                  ♡ A 7 3
                  ◇ K 8 7 2
                  ♣ A K 5 4
  ♠ 3                          ♠ 9 8 6 4
  ♡ J 9 8 5          N         ♡ K Q 10 4 2
  ◇ J 10        W       E      ◇ A Q 9
  ♣ J 10 9 8 3 2      S        ♣ Q
                  ♠ A Q J 10 7 2
                  ♡ 6
                  ◇ 6 5 4 3
                  ♣ 7 6
```

Partner did well not to double four hearts, which is unbeatable on any defence.

PROBLEM 14

♠ K Q 7
♡ 10 8 7 6 3
♦ A 9 4
♣ 6 2

```
      N
   W     E
      S
```

♠ A 8
♡ A K 5
♦ 8 7 3
♣ A 9 7 5 4

Love all.
Dealer North.

The Bidding

WEST	NORTH	EAST	SOUTH
	Pass	Pass	1 NT
Pass	2 ♦*	Pass	2 ♡
Pass	2 NT	Pass	4 ♡
Pass	Pass	Pass	

transfer to hearts

The Lead

West leads the three of clubs and you allow East's queen to hold the first trick. East continues with the ten of clubs and West plays the eight under your ace. How do you plan the play?

Review

The lead was not the most favourable. On any other attack it would have been a simple matter to duck a diamond, subsequently discarding your second diamond loser on the spades and ruffing a diamond with your small trump. With a normal 3–2 trump break this line would have guaranteed your contract.

Solution

Now it is too dangerous to concede a diamond, for if the clubs are 4–2, as seems probable, you may suffer an overruff in clubs and still have to lose a trump trick.

Well, if you can't use your small trump to ruff a diamond you must use it to ruff a spade instead, thereby gaining the extra entry you need to establish a long club.

First cash the ace and king of hearts to guard against promoting an extra trump trick for the defenders. Then ruff a club in dummy, return to the ace of spades and, if necessary, ruff another club. Cash the king of spades, ruff the winning queen of spades in hand, and play your established club for a diamond discard. With 3–2 trumps, your contract is safe unless West can overruff the third spade.

The complete deal:

<pre>
                ♠ K Q 7
                ♡ 10 8 7 6 3
                ◇ A 9 4
                ♣ 6 2
    ♠ 9 4 3   ♠ J 10 6 5 2
    ♡ J 9 2   N   ♡ Q 4
    ◇ Q 10 5   W   E   ◇ K J 6 2
    ♣ K J 8 3   S   ♣ Q 10
                ♠ A 8
                ♡ A K 5
                ◇ 8 7 3
                ♣ A 9 7 5 4
</pre>

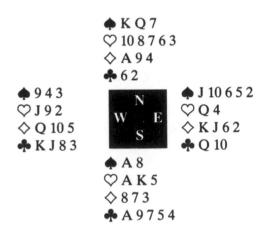

PROBLEM 15

♠ Q 7 5 4
♡ A K 2
♢ A Q 10 6 4
♣ 2

♠ J 10 8 2
♡ 4
Love all.   ♢ J 7 2
Dealer South. ♣ A 8 6 5 3

The Bidding

SOUTH	WEST	NORTH	EAST
Pass	Pass	1 ♢	Pass
1 ♠	Pass	3 ♠	Pass
4 ♠	Pass	Pass	Pass

The Lead

West leads the king of clubs to your ace. How do you plan the play?

Review

This is a borderline game and it looks as though you need to find the trumps 3–2 for a start. Can you afford a losing diamond finesse?

Solution

The danger in playing trumps immediately is that the opponents are sure to force dummy in clubs each time they come in. You will have to enter hand with a heart ruff in order to draw the last trump, and if the diamond finesse fails you may have to lose a club trick as well.

It must be better to test the water by playing a diamond to the ten at trick two. If this wins, it should be safe to switch to trumps. And if the diamond finesse loses, you may still be able to scramble home on a cross-ruff.

The complete deal:

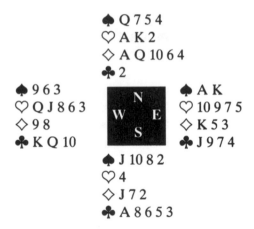

```
              ♠ Q 7 5 4
              ♡ A K 2
              ◇ A Q 10 6 4
              ♣ 2
  ♠ 9 6 3                    ♠ A K
  ♡ Q J 8 6 3     N          ♡ 10 9 7 5
  ◇ 9 8        W     E       ◇ K 5 3
  ♣ K Q 10        S          ♣ J 9 7 4
              ♠ J 10 8 2
              ♡ 4
              ◇ J 7 2
              ♣ A 8 6 5 3
```

In practice East wins with the king of diamonds and returns the suit, hoping to give his partner a ruff. You win in hand, ruff a club in dummy and cash the top hearts, discarding your third diamond. After a heart ruff and another club ruff, you play a diamond from dummy and ruff with the ten of spades. West is unable to overruff and you ruff yet another club in dummy. On the next diamond lead your jack of spades is good for the tenth trick.

PROBLEM 16

♠ K 6 3
♡ A Q
♢ A J 9 5 2
♣ J 5 4

♠ 4
♡ 8 7 6 2
♢ Q 8 6 3
♣ A Q 10 6

E–W game.
Dealer South.

The Bidding

SOUTH	WEST	NORTH	EAST
Pass	1 ◇	1 ♠	2 ♡
Pass	2 NT	Pass	4 ♡
Pass	Pass	Pass	

The Lead

On your lead of the singleton spade partner plays the ace and declarer the seven. North returns the ten of spades and you ruff East's queen. How should you continue?

Review

Declarer is marked with the jack of spades but there seems little chance of getting another spade ruff. In that case the setting tricks will have to come from the minor suits.

Solution

Partner's choice of the spade ten at trick two must have suit-preference implications. He is trying to show that his outside entry lies in diamonds rather than clubs.

A suit-preference signal should not be regarded as a command, of course. You are expected to think for yourself rather than follow instructions blindly. And it may occur to you that a diamond switch is not without danger in this case. If declarer's shape is 3–7–1–2, a diamond return will enable him to set up an extra trick in dummy by ruffing three diamonds in his hand. One of his clubs will disappear on the established diamond and the contract will be made.

There is no need to flirt with disaster. Just return a trump and you will be sure of scoring two tricks in the minor suits at the end.

The complete deal:

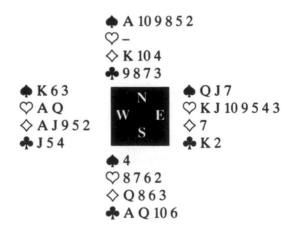

♠ A 10 9 8 5 2
♡ –
♢ K 10 4
♣ 9 8 7 3

♠ K 6 3
♡ A Q
♢ A J 9 5 2
♣ J 5 4

♠ Q J 7
♡ K J 10 9 5 4 3
♢ 7
♣ K 2

♠ 4
♡ 8 7 6 2
♢ Q 8 6 3
♣ A Q 10 6

PROBLEM 17

♠ 9 4 3
♡ 8 2
♦ J 7 3
♣ J 10 7 6 2

♠ A K J 8 6 5 2
♡ A
N–S game. ♦ Q 5
Dealer North. ♣ K Q 5

The Bidding

WEST	NORTH	EAST	SOUTH
	Pass	1 NT*	Dble
2 ♡	Pass	3 ♡	4 ♠
Pass	Pass	Pass	

15–17

The Lead

The queen of hearts is led to your ace. When you play the ace of spades at trick two West discards a heart. How do you continue?

Review

The problem revolves around gaining access to dummy for a trump finesse. East must have all the significant high cards but that doesn't appear to help very much. Have you any ideas?

Solution

Assume in the first place that East has three clubs. If you tackle the clubs immediately, he will hold up the ace until the third round and exit with a heart. You may then try the diamonds, but East will simply play three rounds of the suit. With nothing but trumps left in your hand, you will have to ruff and concede a trump trick.

What about tackling the minors the other way round? It looks no better. East will play two rounds of diamonds and exit in hearts. On winning the third club he will return a diamond, leaving you in the same position as before.

Playing on diamonds first will work when the ace of clubs is doubleton, however. East can take two rounds of diamonds and exit in hearts, but he will be end-played when he wins the second club. This is the only chance, and you should play the queen of diamonds at trick three.

The complete deal:

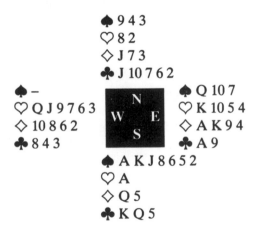

```
              ♠ 9 4 3
              ♡ 8 2
              ♦ J 7 3
              ♣ J 10 7 6 2
♠ -                         ♠ Q 10 7
♡ Q J 9 7 6 3    N          ♡ K 10 5 4
♦ 10 8 6 2    W     E       ♦ A K 9 4
♣ 8 4 3          S          ♣ A 9
              ♠ A K J 8 6 5 2
              ♡ A
              ♦ Q 5
              ♣ K Q 5
```

Note that it would be fatal to play even one round of clubs before the queen of diamonds. Having ducked the first club, East would then take his three minor-suit winners and exit in hearts.

PROBLEM 18

♠ A K
♡ Q 5 3
♢ A J 8 2
♣ Q 9 4 3

♠ 7 6 3
♡ K 7 2
Game all.   ♢ K Q 4
Dealer South.   ♣ A J 6 5

The Bidding

SOUTH	WEST	NORTH	EAST
1 NT	Pass	3 NT	Pass
Pass	Pass		

The Lead

West leads the jack of spades to dummy's king. How do you plan the play?

Review

With seven top tricks you need to develop two more, either both in clubs or one in clubs and one in hearts. And if the spades are 5–3 you can afford to lose the lead only once, otherwise the defenders will develop enough tricks to defeat you. Is there a safe way of playing the hand?

Solution

Only carelessness can bring about your downfall, for the game can be made against any defence and distribution. At trick two you should play a low club to your ace. If nothing exciting happens, return to dummy with the jack of diamonds and play a second club towards your jack. If the clubs are 3–2 there will be no difficulty. If East shows out on the second round, your jack will force out the king and the marked finesse against West will provide the two further club tricks that you need.

And if it is West who has the singleton club? Well, East cannot play his king on the second round without giving you two extra club tricks. When your jack wins and West shows out, you abandon clubs, unblock the diamonds and develop your ninth trick in hearts.

The complete deal:

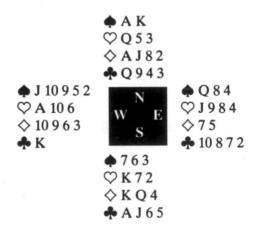

```
                    ♠ A K
                    ♡ Q 5 3
                    ◇ A J 8 2
                    ♣ Q 9 4 3
♠ J 10 9 5 2          N          ♠ Q 8 4
♡ A 10 6                          ♡ J 9 8 4
◇ 10 9 6 3       W       E        ◇ 7 5
♣ K                  S            ♣ 10 8 7 2
                    ♠ 7 6 3
                    ♡ K 7 2
                    ◇ K Q 4
                    ♣ A J 6 5
```

In practice the king of clubs drops under your ace, giving you an easy path to ten tricks.

PROBLEM 19

♠ A 9 3
♡ K Q J 8 4
♢ 6
♣ A 7 4 3

♠ K Q 5
♡ A 9 6 3
Game all.   ♢ A J 7
Dealer South.   ♣ J 10 6

The Bidding

SOUTH	WEST	NORTH	EAST
1 NT	Pass	2 ♢*	Pass
2 ♡	Pass	3 ♣	Pass
4 ♡	Pass	4 ♠	Pass
6 ♡	Pass	Pass	Pass

transfer to hearts

The Lead

West attacks with the seven of spades. You play low from dummy and capture East's ten with your king. When you play a low heart to the king West discards a spade. How should you continue?

Review

You are in a position to pick up the trumps, but it looks as though you need to find one of the defenders with a doubleton honour in clubs if you are to avoid two losers in the suit. What is the best way to proceed?

Solution

Since East has the heart length he is the one who is likely to have the doubleton club. But if you play a low club from dummy at trick three you may have difficulty with your entries. You need to ruff two diamonds in dummy, remember, and it must be right to take one of those ruffs immediately.

Play a diamond to your ace, ruff a diamond on the table, and *then* play a low club away from the ace. If East wins and returns a spade you can win with the queen, ruff your third diamond high, and draw trumps with the help of a finesse. Now you rely on the club finesse for your twelfth trick.

The complete deal:

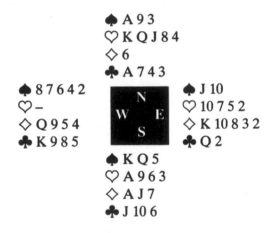

```
              ♠ A 9 3
              ♡ K Q J 8 4
              ◇ 6
              ♣ A 7 4 3
♠ 8 7 6 4 2         N          ♠ J 10
♡ –                           ♡ 10 7 5 2
◇ Q 9 5 4     W       E        ◇ K 10 8 3 2
♣ K 9 8 5          S          ♣ Q 2
              ♠ K Q 5
              ♡ A 9 6 3
              ◇ A J 7
              ♣ J 10 6
```

If you concede the club prematurely at trick three a spade will come back, and you will be unable to negotiate two diamond ruffs without running into an enemy ruff in one of the black suits.

PROBLEM 20

♠ 10 9 5 2
♡ K Q 7 4 2
◇ J 9 5
♣ A

```
        N
    W       E
        S
```

♠ K Q
♡ J 5

Love all.   ◇ Q 10 6 2
Dealer South.   ♣ Q J 7 4 3

The Bidding

SOUTH	WEST	NORTH	EAST
Pass	Pass	Pass	1 ♡
Pass	4 ♡	Pass	Pass
Pass			

The Lead

On your lead of the king of spades partner plays the eight and declarer the three. You continue with the queen of spades, North playing the four and East the six. What now?

Review

It looks as though declarer has a further spade loser, but partner will need a high card in one of the red suits if the contract is to be defeated. Is it an occasion for passive defence?

[47]

Solution

In the unlikely event of partner having the ace of hearts you have nothing to worry about. Partner's high card is more likely to be in diamonds, however, and you cannot afford to play a passive game. Suppose declarer started with the ace and another diamond and three spades headed by the jack. On a passive trump or club return he will draw trumps and lead the jack of spades, and his losing diamond will eventually go away on dummy's fourth spade.

The lead of a low diamond at trick three will fare no better. The nine will draw partner's king and the ace will win. After drawing trumps declarer will play his second diamond, and his spade loser will disappear on the jack of diamonds.

You need to establish a diamond trick for partner rather than for yourself, and the correct move is to lead the queen of diamonds at trick three. If declarer has the critical holding this will render him helpless. Whether he wins or ducks he will be unable to avoid the loss of a diamond and a spade.

The complete deal:

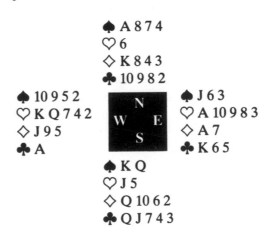

```
              ♠ A 8 7 4
              ♡ 6
              ◇ K 8 4 3
              ♣ 10 9 8 2
♠ 10 9 5 2        N        ♠ J 6 3
♡ K Q 7 4 2   W     E      ♡ A 10 9 8 3
◇ J 9 5           S        ◇ A 7
♣ A                        ♣ K 6 5
              ♠ K Q
              ♡ J 5
              ◇ Q 10 6 2
              ♣ Q J 7 4 3
```

PROBLEM 21

♠ 8 5
♡ K Q 3
◇ Q J 9 3
♣ A J 7 4

♠ A J 10
♡ A 8 2
◇ K 5 4
♣ Q 10 3 2

E–W game.
Dealer South.

The Bidding

SOUTH	WEST	NORTH	EAST
1 ♣	Pass	1 ◇	Pass
1 NT	Pass	3 NT	Pass
Pass	Pass		

The Lead

West leads the king of spades and East plays the two. How do you plan the play?

Review

It is comforting to have a double stopper in spades, but your contract will still be in danger if West has a five-card suit, as seems likely. You have to look for maximum safety.

Solution

It would be unwise to win the first spade and take an immediate club finesse. Nor is it safe to win the first trick and lead a diamond from hand. East may win and return a spade which West can duck. Now if the diamond ten fails to drop and the club finesse loses you are sunk.

What about trying a Bath Coup by playing the ten of spades at trick one? West will no doubt switch to clubs, and you can go up with the ace and play on diamonds. If you keep the ace of spades for the third round, you will be home when the spades are 5–3 and East has the club king. But you cannot be sure that East has the club king, and the spades may be 4–4.

There is a line of play that is almost completely safe. Win the first trick, cross to the queen of hearts and lead the low diamond. If East plays the ace you have nine tricks, while if the king of diamonds is allowed to win you can switch to clubs.

It is unlikely that West will have the diamond ace since he failed to overcall, but if he does capture the king of diamonds and return a low spade you will know that East has the club king. You can then exit with your third spade, hoping to squeeze East in the minors at the end.

The complete deal:

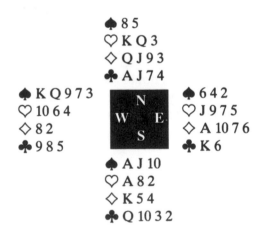

```
                ♠ 8 5
                ♡ K Q 3
                ◇ Q J 9 3
                ♣ A J 7 4
  ♠ K Q 9 7 3                ♠ 6 4 2
  ♡ 10 6 4          N        ♡ J 9 7 5
  ◇ 8 2         W       E    ◇ A 10 7 6
  ♣ 9 8 5           S        ♣ K 6
                ♠ A J 10
                ♡ A 8 2
                ◇ K 5 4
                ♣ Q 10 3 2
```

PROBLEM 22

♠ A Q 6 2
♡ J 6 5
◇ A 4
♣ 10 7 4 3

♠ 10 5
♡ A K Q 8 3
◇ J 7
♣ A 8 5 2

N–S game.
Dealer South.

The Bidding

SOUTH	WEST	NORTH	EAST
1 ♡	Pass	1 ♠	Pass
2 ♣	Pass	3 ♡	Pass
4 ♡	Pass	Pass	Pass

The Lead

West leads the two of diamonds and you play low from dummy. East wins with the queen and returns a diamond to the ace. How do you plan the play?

Review

There are eight top tricks, and on a normal split you can expect a ninth trick from the clubs. For the tenth trick it looks as though you will have to rely on the spade finesse. Is there a way of giving yourself an extra chance?

Solution

There is a possibility that the club suit will be blocked, and you can take advantage of this by playing for a partial elimination. You have already taken a step in the right direction by ducking the first round of diamonds.

Draw just two rounds of trumps with the ace and jack, then play a club to the ace and continue with a second club. If East has to win this trick and has no trump to return, you will not need the spade finesse after all. East will have to return a spade into the tenace or play a diamond, enabling you to discard your losing spade as you ruff in dummy.

The complete deal:

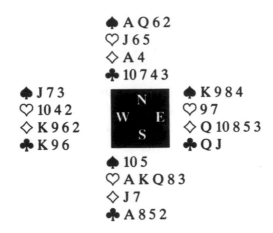

On the lie of the cards there is no escape from the partial elimination and throw-in.

PROBLEM 23

♠ 10 6 2
♡ J 5
♦ K 9
♣ A K Q 10 8 4

♠ A Q 8 3
♡ Q 8 3
♦ A 6 5 4
♣ 6 2

N–S game.
Dealer West.

The Bidding

WEST	NORTH	EAST	SOUTH
1 ♠	2 ♣	Pass	2 NT
3 ♡	3 NT	Pass	Pass
Pass			

The Lead

West leads the ten of hearts to the five, two and queen. Both defenders follow with small cards when you play a club to the ace. How should you continue?

Review

If the clubs break 3–2 you will score at least ten tricks, but a 4–1 club break may result in the opponents cashing five tricks before you can make nine. What can you do about it?

Solution

There is no need to rely entirely on the club suit. The bidding marks West with at least ten cards in the majors and, since he has already shown one club, he cannot have more than two diamonds. Just play off the ace and king of diamonds and then exit with a heart.

West is welcome to cash his four hearts, on which you can discard two spades and a club from dummy and a spade and a diamond from your hand. Then, if he has no clubs left, West will have to present you with an eighth trick by leading a spade into your tenace. The ninth trick will materialise when you cash the second spade winner, squeezing East in the minor suits.

The complete deal:

```
              ♠ 10 6 2
              ♡ J 5
              ◇ K 9
              ♣ A K Q 10 8 4
♠ K J 9 5 4                    ♠ 7
♡ A K 10 9 6      N           ♡ 7 4 2
◇ 10 8        W       E       ◇ Q J 7 3 2
♣ 5              S            ♣ J 9 7 3
              ♠ A Q 8 3
              ♡ Q 8 3
              ◇ A 6 5 4
              ♣ 6 2
```

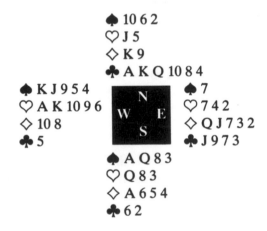

PROBLEM 24

♠ Q 7 4
♡ K Q 5
◇ Q J 6 5
♣ A Q J

```
      N
  W       E
      S
```

♠ K J 8 5 2
♡ 3
◇ A K 9 7 4
♣ 8 5

E–W game.
Dealer South.

The Bidding

SOUTH	WEST	NORTH	EAST
1 ♠	1 NT	2 ♠	3 ♡
3 ♠	4 ♡	Pass	Pass
Pass			

The Lead

On your lead of the ace of diamonds North plays the three and East the eight. How should you continue?

Review

From the play to the first trick it appears that the missing diamonds are divided 2–2, and it is clear that you must take your outside tricks before declarer can get discards on the diamonds. What is the correct switch?

Solution

Partner is likely to have one high card, which may be in spades, clubs or trumps. There can be no hurry for a spade switch if partner has the ace, for you will have a second chance to lead spades when you are in with the king of diamonds. A club switch is unlikely to work even if partner has the king. Declarer will go up with the ace, draw trumps, and establish the diamonds for a spade discard.

By a process of elimination you are forced to the conclusion that a trump switch is needed if you are to retain all your options. If partner has the ace of trumps he will return a spade to set up the fourth defensive trick.

The complete deal:

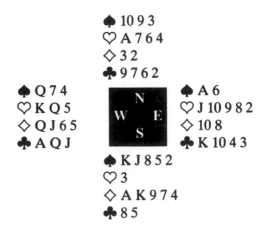

```
                      ♠ 10 9 3
                      ♡ A 7 6 4
                      ◇ 3 2
                      ♣ 9 7 6 2
        ♠ Q 7 4              N          ♠ A 6
        ♡ K Q 5         W         E     ♡ J 10 9 8 2
        ◇ Q J 6 5            S          ◇ 10 8
        ♣ A Q J                         ♣ K 10 4 3
                      ♠ K J 8 5 2
                      ♡ 3
                      ◇ A K 9 7 4
                      ♣ 8 5
```

PROBLEM 25

♠ 2
♡ A J 7 4 3 2
♢ Q 7
♣ 10 9 8 7

♠ J 9 6 5
♡ 6
♢ K 9 3
♣ A K Q J 2

Game all.
Dealer South.

The Bidding

SOUTH	WEST	NORTH	EAST
1 ♣	Dble	2 ♡	2 ♠
Pass	3 ♠	4 ♣	Pass
Pass	Pass		

The Lead

West leads the king of hearts to dummy's ace, East following with the eight. You continue with a small heart and ruff high, but the prospect of establishing the suit vanishes when East discards the two of diamonds. How should you continue?

Review

With only two tricks in the side suits you need eight tricks from the trumps. How do you time the cross-ruff?

Solution

You are lucky to have escaped an initial trump lead, but you can be sure that the defenders will return a trump each time you let them in. This means that you cannot afford to give up an early trick in both diamonds and spades, which in turn creates entry problems in dummy. If you could slip past the ace of diamonds you would be all right, for you could then concede a spade trick.

West is likely to have the ace of diamonds, but there is no need to bank on this. The safe play at trick three is the king of diamonds from hand. If either defender wins and returns a trump, you can win in dummy, ruff a heart, cross to the queen of diamonds, ruff another heart, return to dummy with a diamond ruff and ruff a further heart with your last trump.

If the king of diamonds is allowed to win at trick three, of course, you simply concede a spade and then cross-ruff for ten tricks.

The complete deal:

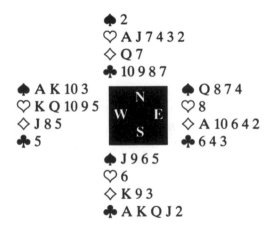

```
                  ♠ 2
                  ♡ A J 7 4 3 2
                  ♢ Q 7
                  ♣ 10 9 8 7
   ♠ A K 10 3                ♠ Q 8 7 4
   ♡ K Q 10 9 5      N       ♡ 8
   ♢ J 8 5       W       E   ♢ A 10 6 4 2
   ♣ 5               S       ♣ 6 4 3
                  ♠ J 9 6 5
                  ♡ 6
                  ♢ K 9 3
                  ♣ A K Q J 2
```

PROBLEM 26

♠ 7 5
♡ A K J
◇ A 10 5
♣ J 9 7 6 3

♠ A K Q 3
♡ Q 9 7 6 2
Game all.   ◇ 9 6 4
Dealer North.   ♣ A

The Bidding

WEST	NORTH	EAST	SOUTH
	1 NT	Pass	2 ♣
Pass	2 ◇	Pass	3 ♡
Pass	4 ◇	Pass	6 ♡
Pass	Pass	Pass	

The Lead

West leads the king of clubs to your ace, East following with the two. How do you plan the play?

Review

This is not the greatest of slams. There are only five outside winners, and even if you can develop a long club you will need six tricks from the trumps. How should you proceed?

Solution

Setting up a long club may work if the suit breaks 4–3 and if the trumps are 3–2, but you will need to risk ruffing the fourth club with the nine of hearts. If you are going to do that you may as well play on cross-ruff lines, ruffing four clubs in hand and aiming for seven trump tricks. The advantage is that you may then succeed against a 4–1 trump break.

To get the timing right you should duck a diamond at trick two. Win the trump return in dummy, ruff a club, cash the top spades for a diamond discard, cross to the ace of diamonds and ruff another club. Ruff a diamond on the table and ruff the fourth club with the nine of hearts. When that stands up you make the last two tricks by ruffing with master trumps.

The complete deal:

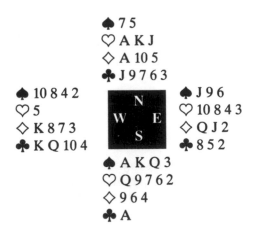

♠ 7 5
♡ A K J
♢ A 10 5
♣ J 9 7 6 3

♠ 10 8 4 2
♡ 5
♢ K 8 7 3
♣ K Q 10 4

♠ J 9 6
♡ 10 8 4 3
♢ Q J 2
♣ 8 5 2

♠ A K Q 3
♡ Q 9 7 6 2
♢ 9 6 4
♣ A

Instead of ducking a diamond at trick two you can play four rounds of spades, discarding two diamonds from the table. The vital point is to prepare your cross-ruff before drawing a round of trumps.

An initial trump lead would have defeated the slam.

PROBLEM 27

♠ A 5 3
♡ A 9 4 2
♢ K
♣ A K Q 8 5

♠ Q 6
♡ 10 6 5 3
♢ A J 9 6 2
♣ 6 2

N–S game.
Dealer North.

The Bidding

WEST	NORTH	EAST	SOUTH
	1 ♣	Pass	1 ♢
1 ♡	2 ♡	Pass	2 NT
Pass	3 NT	Pass	Pass
Pass			

The Lead

The opening lead is the king of hearts. You play low from dummy and East discards the jack of spades. West switches to the four of spades and you capture East's eight with your queen. When you test the clubs West discards a diamond on the second round. How should you continue?

Review

Two tricks in each of the red suits would see you home, but the blockage in diamonds is a nuisance. How might you overcome this?

Solution

You need to plan a throw-in against West, but first you will have to remove his exit cards in spades. Unblock the king of diamonds and continue with the low spade from dummy. On winning the spade return you can cash the queen of clubs and then play the nine of hearts from the table. Now, if West is out of spades as seems likely, he is trapped. If he wins this trick his red-suit return will give you an easy passage. If West allows the nine of hearts to hold, you simply continue with the ace and another heart. West is welcome to score his heart tricks, for he must concede a trick to the ace of diamonds at the end.

The complete deal:

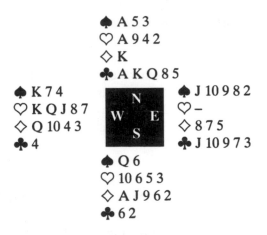

♠ A 5 3
♡ A 9 4 2
♢ K
♣ A K Q 8 5

♠ K 7 4
♡ K Q J 8 7
♢ Q 10 4 3
♣ 4

♠ J 10 9 8 2
♡ –
♢ 8 7 5
♣ J 10 9 7 3

♠ Q 6
♡ 10 6 5 3
♢ A J 9 6 2
♣ 6 2

It's lucky for you that West decided to enter the bidding. Otherwise partner might have been toiling in four hearts.

PROBLEM 28

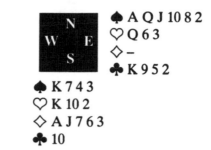

♠ A Q J 10 8 2
♡ Q 6 3
♢ –
♣ K 9 5 2

♠ K 7 4 3
♡ K 10 2
♢ A J 7 6 3
♣ 10

Game all.
Dealer North.

The Bidding

WEST	NORTH	EAST	SOUTH
	Pass	1 ♠	Pass
2 ♡	Pass	4 ♡	Pass
5 ♣	Pass	5 ♢	Pass
6 ♡	Pass	Pass	Pass

The Lead

North leads the two of diamonds which is ruffed in dummy with the three of hearts. The queen of hearts is led, and when you cover with the king you are allowed to hold the trick, West playing the four and North the seven. What do you lead now?

Review

Declarer has preserved control by conceding your trump trick at a moment when dummy can still take care of a diamond return. How might you embarrass him?

Solution

You have to ask yourself where the declarer is going for tricks. The answer lies on the table. It is inconceivable that West can make twelve tricks without the help of dummy's long spades.

Think for a moment about the spade position. Holding a singleton spade partner might well have chosen that as his opening lead, so it is long odds that declarer has the singleton. In that case it must be a good idea to cut the link before trumps can be drawn. You should lead a small spade at trick three.

The complete deal:

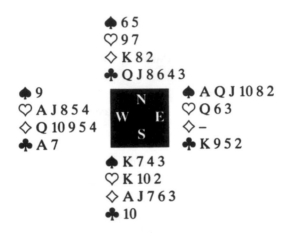

```
                    ♠ 6 5
                    ♡ 9 7
                    ◇ K 8 2
                    ♣ Q J 8 6 4 3
    ♠ 9                         ♠ A Q J 10 8 2
    ♡ A J 8 5 4                 ♡ Q 6 3
    ◇ Q 10 9 5 4                ◇ -
    ♣ A 7                       ♣ K 9 5 2
                    ♠ K 7 4 3
                    ♡ K 10 2
                    ◇ A J 7 6 3
                    ♣ 10
```

Declarer will not be amused by your spade return, for it forces him to rely on a 3–3 spade break. The best he can do is win with the nine, ruff a diamond, run the queen of spades, cross to hand with the ace of clubs and draw trumps. But that is only eleven tricks.

On any other return declarer easily makes the slam, drawing trumps and establishing the spades with the aid of a ruffing finesse.

PROBLEM 29

♠ 10 5 4
♡ J 10 3
◇ A 9 2
♣ A Q 10 8

♠ K J 6 2
♡ A K
◇ K Q 4 3
♣ J 9 4

E–W game.
Dealer North.

The Bidding

WEST	NORTH	EAST	SOUTH
	Pass	Pass	1 NT
Pass	3 NT	Pass	Pass
Pass			

The Lead

West leads the five of hearts to the jack, two and ace. How do you plan the play?

Review

There will always be nine tricks if the club finesse is right or if the diamonds break 3–3. But after a losing club finesse you will not have time to try for a spade trick, since the play to the first trick forewarns of a 5–3 heart split. How do you make the most of your chances?

Solution

You should not be in a hurry to take that dangerous club finesse. First test the diamonds by cashing the king followed by the queen. If both defenders follow suit it will be safe to continue with a third diamond to the ace. On a 3–3 diamond break you can make sure of your contract by playing a small club from dummy.

If someone shows out on the third diamond you can give yourself a small extra chance by continuing with a low spade, hoping to find a favourable position. If East plays low you will put up the king, and if this loses you will have to fall back on the club finesse.

The complete deal:

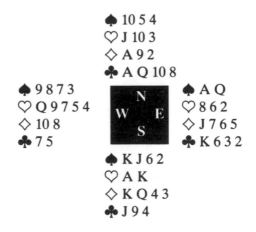

                    ♠ 10 5 4
                    ♡ J 10 3
                    ◇ A 9 2
                    ♣ A Q 10 8
    ♠ 9 8 7 3   ♠ A Q
    ♡ Q 9 7 5 4   ♡ 8 6 2
    ◇ 10 8   ◇ J 7 6 5
    ♣ 7 5   ♣ K 6 3 2
                    ♠ K J 6 2
                    ♡ A K
                    ◇ K Q 4 3
                    ♣ J 9 4

In practice West discards a club on the third diamond. East goes up with the ace of spades to cash his diamond winner. West discards a club and you carefully throw a club from dummy. You win the heart return and hit the jackpot when you cash the king of spades. Now the hand is an open book. When you play a club to the ace West has to throw a heart, whereupon you cash the spade ten and exit with the heart ten, using West's hearts as stepping-stones to reach your stranded jack of spades.

PROBLEM 30

♠ Q 5
♡ A K 10 3
◇ Q 10
♣ A Q 7 6 2

♠ A 7 4 3
♡ J 7 5 2
Love all.   ◇ A K J
Dealer North.   ♣ 8 3

The Bidding

WEST	NORTH	EAST	SOUTH
	1 ♣	Pass	1 ♡
Pass	3 ♡	Pass	3 NT
Pass	Pass	Pass	

The Lead

West leads the jack of spades and dummy's queen is covered by the king. East returns the two of spades to his partner's nine, and West continues with the spade ten. You discard a club from dummy, East follows with the six of spades and you take your ace. A finesse of the ten of hearts succeeds, but when you cash the king of hearts East discards a club. What now?

Review

Four hearts would have been easier in spite of the 4–1 break. Three no-trumps is by no means secure. At the moment you have only eight tricks and it looks as though the ninth trick will need to come from clubs. Does this mean that you have to bank on the club finesse?

Solution

The club finesse is not very likely to succeed. The defensive carding indicates that East has the outstanding spade, and he must have four clubs since he has already discarded one. East's pattern is likely to be 4–1–4–4, and you must plan to throw him in with the fourth spade.

But the throw-in will not be effective as long as East retains an exit card in diamonds. First you must cash the ace of hearts to force another discard from East. If he parts with a second club, you can enter hand with a diamond and take the club finesse, expecting to make a second club trick even if the king is off-side. If East discards a diamond, as he probably will, you take three rounds of diamonds before exiting with the spade.

The complete deal:

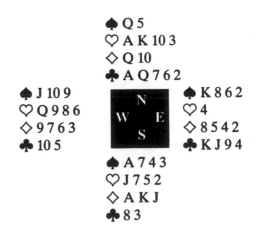

```
                    ♠ Q 5
                    ♡ A K 10 3
                    ♦ Q 10
                    ♣ A Q 7 6 2
  ♠ J 10 9                        ♠ K 8 6 2
  ♡ Q 9 8 6           N           ♡ 4
  ♦ 9 7 6 3      W         E       ♦ 8 5 4 2
  ♣ 10 5             S            ♣ K J 9 4
                    ♠ A 7 4 3
                    ♡ J 7 5 2
                    ♦ A K J
                    ♣ 8 3
```

PROBLEM 31

♠ K 6
♡ 10 8 6
◇ J 9 6 5
♣ A Q J 5

♠ 9 7 5
♡ A K 7 5 3 2
Game all.   ◇ –
Dealer West. ♣ K 7 6 2

The Bidding

WEST	NORTH	EAST	SOUTH
Pass	Pass	1 ◇	1 ♡
Pass	2 ◇	2 ♠	3 ♡
Pass	4 ♡	Pass	Pass
Pass			

The Lead

West leads the four of hearts to the six, nine and king. How do you plan the play?

Review

This lead looks like a singleton and is distinctly unfriendly. On any other attack you could have expected to ruff your third spade in dummy. Now there is a danger of losing three spades and a trump. What can you do about it?

Solution

There is no point in leading a spade since East is marked with the ace. Each time he comes in he will play trumps, leaving you with four losers.

East's shape is likely to be 4–3–5–1. If he has all the top diamonds you may be able to engineer an end-play against him by playing for a partial dummy reversal. Cash the ace of hearts to check the position, and continue with the king and another club. East cannot afford to ruff, for this would enable you to ruff a spade in dummy after all. On the table with the club jack, you ruff a diamond, return to the queen of clubs, ruff another diamond and play a club to the ace. East meanwhile is sure to have trouble with his discards. He can afford to throw two spades on the clubs, but at this point he has to part with a diamond. You ruff another diamond and exit with your last trump. East can cash one high diamond and the ace of spades, but he has to yield the last trick to the spade king.

The complete deal:

♠ K 6
♡ 10 8 6
◇ J 9 6 5
♣ A Q J 5

♠ J 10 3 2   ♠ A Q 8 4
♡ 4   ♡ Q J 9
◇ 10 7 3 2   ◇ A K Q 8 4
♣ 10 9 8 4   ♣ 3

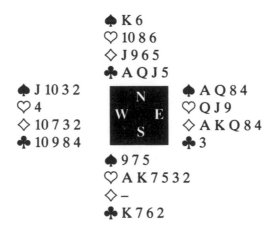

♠ 9 7 5
♡ A K 7 5 3 2
◇ –
♣ K 7 6 2

The play of the last club squeezed East in three suits including trumps. It's called a knockout strip-squeeze.

PROBLEM 32

♠ 7 6 4 3
♡ J 9
♦ A 10 4
♣ A K J 9

N
W E
S

♠ A 10 5
♡ Q 7 6 5 3
♦ K Q
♣ 10 8 4

N–S game.
Dealer West.

The Bidding

WEST	NORTH	EAST	SOUTH
1 ♣	Pass	2 NT	Pass
3 NT	Pass	Pass	Pass

The Lead

On your lead of the five of hearts dummy plays the nine, North the two and East the ten. Declarer leads the three of diamonds on which you play the queen, dummy the four and North the two. Winning the next heart with the ace, East leads the five of diamonds to the king, ten and nine. What now?

Review

The obvious move is to clear the hearts while you still have the ace of spades as an entry. Is there a case for doing something different?

Solution

Declarer is marked with five diamonds, and his line of play strongly suggests that he has the queen of clubs as a re-entry. In that case a further heart will do you no good. East will win, unblock the ace of diamonds, return to the queen of clubs and make ten tricks.

What about a spade switch? It is possible for partner to have the king and the jack, but an immediate spade switch will be necessary only when declarer has the doubleton queen, which must be against the odds. East is likely to have three spades and, to judge from the care he has taken to keep your partner off lead, he may well have the king.

If declarer *has* three spades (and therefore two clubs) you can defeat the contract irrespective of whether his spade honour is the queen or the king. A club lead at this point will play havoc with the communications. No matter where declarer wins the trick, he will have to abandon two winners in one hand or the other. Eventually he will have to play spades himself, and the defenders will take five tricks.

The complete deal:

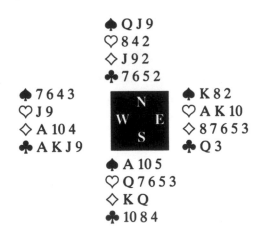

```
                    ♠ Q J 9
                    ♡ 8 4 2
                    ◇ J 9 2
                    ♣ 7 6 5 2
  ♠ 7 6 4 3                        ♠ K 8 2
  ♡ J 9             N             ♡ A K 10
  ◇ A 10 4     W         E        ◇ 8 7 6 5 3
  ♣ A K J 9          S            ♣ Q 3
                    ♠ A 10 5
                    ♡ Q 7 6 5 3
                    ◇ K Q
                    ♣ 10 8 4
```

PROBLEM 33

♠ J 6 5 4 2
♡ Q 9 8
♦ K Q
♣ A 8 6

♠ A 7 3
♡ A K 10 7 6 5 4
N–S game.　　♦ –
Dealer North.　♣ K 7 5

The Bidding

WEST	NORTH	EAST	SOUTH
	1 ♠	Pass	2 ♡
3 ♦	3 ♡	5 ♦	6 ♡
Pass	Pass	Pass	

The Lead

West leads the ace of diamonds. How do you plan the play?

Review

The friendly lead helps to compensate for the unsuitable dummy. You will be able to dispose of one of your spade losers and you can hope to set up the spade suit. How should you tackle the hand?

Solution

It seems obvious to ruff the diamond lead, draw trumps in two rounds, discard a spade on the king of diamonds and then play the ace and another spade. A 3–2 break will enable you to establish the suit for a discard of your losing club.

On the bidding, however, a 4–1 spade break is quite likely, and it is better to use your entries in a different order. Ruff the initial diamond, cross to the ace of clubs and take your spade discard on the diamond king. Then, before touching trumps, play the ace and another spade. If the suit breaks 3–2 you will have no problems. And if the spades prove to be 4–1 you will still have a chance. After winning the club return you can lead a small trump and insert the eight. If this wins, you ruff a spade high, enter dummy with a second trump and ruff another spade high. A third trump puts dummy in to cash the long spade for a club discard.

The complete deal:

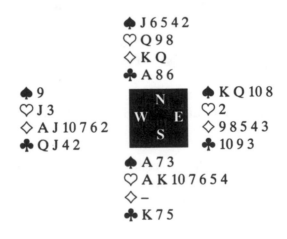

```
                  ♠ J 6 5 4 2
                  ♡ Q 9 8
                  ♢ K Q
                  ♣ A 8 6
  ♠ 9                              ♠ K Q 10 8
  ♡ J 3              N             ♡ 2
  ♢ A J 10 7 6 2  W     E          ♢ 9 8 5 4 3
  ♣ Q J 4 2          S             ♣ 10 9 3
                  ♠ A 7 3
                  ♡ A K 10 7 6 5 4
                  ♢ -
                  ♣ K 7 5
```

PROBLEM 34

♠ A 8 4
♡ 3
♢ A J 6 5
♣ A K Q 10 3

♠ K 7 2
♡ A J 7

N–S game.
Dealer North.

♢ K Q 9 3
♣ 9 7 6

The Bidding

WEST	NORTH	EAST	SOUTH
	1 ♣	Pass	1 ♢
Pass	4 ♢	Pass	4 ♡
Pass	4 ♠	Pass	6 ♢
Pass	Pass	Pass	

The Lead

West leads the nine of hearts to the queen and ace. How do you plan the play?

Review

It looks as though you may have underbid this hand. Normal breaks in the minor suits will certainly produce thirteen tricks. So perhaps it is a suitable occasion for trying to protect yourself against bad breaks.

Solution

You might ruff a heart at trick two, then cash the ace of diamonds and continue with a second diamond to your king. If trumps are 3–2 you will be able to ruff the other heart loser, return to the king of spades, draw the last trump, and make your contract irrespective of the club division. But if the trumps are 4–1 this line will leave you dependent on a 3–2 club break.

With the position of the king of hearts marked on your right, it is possible to cater for 4–1 breaks in both minor suits. Just ruff the small heart in dummy and continue with the ace, jack and another trump, drawing the fourth round if necessary. Then test the clubs by playing the ace and king. If East shows out, return to the king of spades and take the marked finesse for thirteen tricks.

If it is West who shows out on the second club, the play of the ace of spades followed by the king will force East to bare his king of hearts. He can then be thrown in with the heart to lead into the club tenace.

The complete deal:

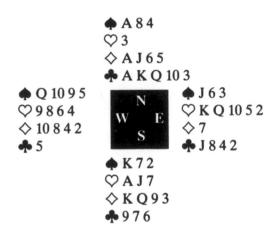

♠ A 8 4
♡ 3
♦ A J 6 5
♣ A K Q 10 3

♠ Q 10 9 5
♡ 9 8 6 4
♦ 10 8 4 2
♣ 5

♠ J 6 3
♡ K Q 10 5 2
♦ 7
♣ J 8 4 2

♠ K 7 2
♡ A J 7
♦ K Q 9 3
♣ 9 7 6

PROBLEM 35

♠ K 9 7 4
♡ A 4 3
◇ 10 7 6
♣ 7 6 3

♠ A J 8 6 2
♡ K 6 2
◇ A K Q 2
♣ A

E–W game.
Dealer North.

The Bidding

WEST	NORTH	EAST	SOUTH
	Pass	Pass	2 ♣
Pass	2 NT	Pass	3 ♠
Pass	4 ♡	Pass	6 ♠
Pass	Pass	Pass	

The Lead

West leads the five of diamonds and dummy's ten wins the trick, East following with the three. How do you plan the play?

Review

Prospects are bright now that you are assured of four diamond tricks. It will be easy if the trumps are no worse than 3–1, for dummy's heart loser will disappear on your fourth diamond. Is there any way of overcoming a 4–0 trump split?

Solution

The standard safety play to avoid the loss of more than one trump with this holding is to start with a low card to the ace. It will not do in this case, however. If either defender shows out on the first round, you will have no way of avoiding a loser in both trumps and hearts.

Should you then start with the king of spades, which will at least cater for the possibility of a void in the West hand?

No. There is a completely safe way of playing the hand. Play a club to your ace at trick two and continue with a low spade from hand. If West shows out the play is easy. And if West plays a low spade you can insert the seven from dummy, making sure of the slam whether East can win or not.

The complete deal:

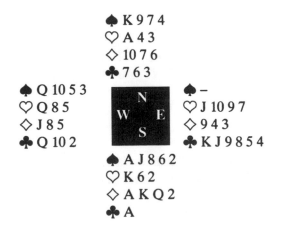

If West inserts the ten of spades and East shows out under dummy's king, you are in a position to organise a dummy reversal. Ruff a club and then offer West the jack of spades. No matter what he returns, you can ruff the third club in your hand to bring home the slam.

PROBLEM 36

♠ 10 8 6 3
♡ K J 4
◇ A K 8 5 2
♣ 3

	N	
W		E
	S	

♠ A K J 7 4 2
♡ A Q 3
Love all.　　　◇ 4
Dealer South.　♣ 10 5 4

The Bidding

SOUTH	WEST	NORTH	EAST
1 ♠	Pass	Pass	3 ♣
Pass	3 ◇	Pass	3 ♡
Pass	3 ♠	Pass	3 NT
Pass	Pass	Pass	

The Lead

On your lead of the ace of spades partner discards the three of diamonds. Two queens appear when you continue with the king of spades – the queen of diamonds from North and the queen of spades from East. What now?

Review

The play to the second trick is intriguing. Why has East made you a present of an extra trick by unblocking the queen of spades? Can you work out his distribution?

Solution

You may be sure that East is not out to do you any favours. He must be desperate for an entry to dummy, which can only mean he has no diamonds. His distribution must be 3–4–0–6, presumably with solid clubs. In that case it will not do to continue spades. East will win in dummy, cash the top diamonds, and run the clubs to make his contract.

What about a diamond switch? No, that won't work if declarer cashes both top diamonds before running the clubs. You will have to come down to three cards and you will be forced to yield a further trick to dummy in the end-game.

To defeat this contract you must arrange for dummy to come under pressure before you do, and the way to achieve that is by switching to a club at trick three. On the run of the clubs you can discard your diamond and two spades, but dummy will have no card to spare on the sixth club.

The complete deal:

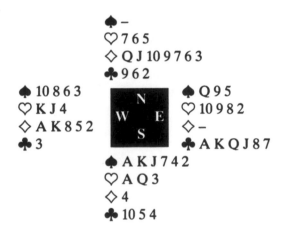

```
              ♠ –
              ♡ 7 6 5
              ◇ Q J 10 9 7 6 3
              ♣ 9 6 2
  ♠ 10 8 6 3        N        ♠ Q 9 5
  ♡ K J 4                    ♡ 10 9 8 2
  ◇ A K 8 5 2    W     E     ◇ –
  ♣ 3                S       ♣ A K Q J 8 7
              ♠ A K J 7 4 2
              ♡ A Q 3
              ◇ 4
              ♣ 10 5 4
```

In practice declarer will probably run only five clubs and then lead a heart or a spade, but you have an answer to anything he may try.

TEST YOUR CARD PLAY

VOLUME 2

INTRODUCTION

This is the second volume in my new series of quiz-books, and the formula is the same as before. Not all of the problems are original. Some have been taken from *Test Your Match Play*, *The Tough Game* and *The Needle Match*, books which are now out of print. A new generation of readers will not have seen these hands, and in any case there are enough fresh problems here to whet the most jaded appetite.

The problems are set on odd-numbered pages with only two hands on view. A bidding sequence is supplied in every case, but the bidding is important only in so far as it provides a clue to the nature of the opponents' holdings. The opening lead is specified, and in some cases the play to the first few tricks is given. At this point you are invited to take over. Try to work out the best line of play or defence for yourself before reading on. In case of difficulty, you may find some inspiration in the next paragraph where the options are reviewed and the issues clarified. The solution and the complete deal are given overleaf.

The hands have been arranged in no particular order except that they have been roughly graded according to difficulty, the easier ones coming in the earlier part of the book. You can regard your card play as satisfactory if you come up with the right answer to twenty or more of these problems. Twenty-five correct is an excellent score, thirty is magnificent and thirty-five unbelievable. Good luck!

PROBLEM 1

♠ 10 5 3
♡ Q 8
♦ K Q 10 3
♣ J 8 5 4

N–S game.
Dealer South.

♠ K Q 9 7
♡ K 9 5
♦ A J 2
♣ A 10 9

The Bidding

SOUTH	WEST	NORTH	EAST
1 ♠	Pass	2 ♣	Pass
2 NT	Pass	3 NT	Pass
Pass	Pass		

The Lead

West leads the queen of clubs to the four, three and ace. On enquiry you are told that the queen may be from a short king-queen suit. How do you plan the play?

Review

The lead appears to have given you a useful extra tempo. You can count three club tricks, four diamonds, and at least one trick in each of the majors. Do you see any hazards?

[85]

Solution

You may have to lose the lead twice to establish your tricks, and a heart switch by West when he gains the lead could put the contract at risk. You have no clue to the location of the spade ace, but it is a safe bet that West will have the club king. He would hardly have led the club queen from Q x.

The temptation to continue clubs at trick two must be resisted. Play a diamond to the ten and return a spade, putting up the king if East plays low. If this wins, you can switch to clubs and make sure of nine tricks. If East takes the ace of spades and switches to a heart he can do no harm, while if West has the ace of spades and East the ace of hearts you may have to bank on a second-round finesse of the spade ten.

The complete deal:

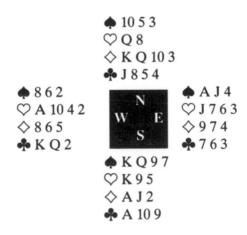

```
              ♠ 10 5 3
              ♡ Q 8
              ◇ K Q 10 3
              ♣ J 8 5 4
♠ 8 6 2                        ♠ A J 4
♡ A 10 4 2        N           ♡ J 7 6 3
◇ 8 6 5        W     E        ◇ 9 7 4
♣ K Q 2           S           ♣ 7 6 3
              ♠ K Q 9 7
              ♡ K 9 5
              ◇ A J 2
              ♣ A 10 9
```

You can see what will happen if you continue clubs at trick two. West wins and switches to the two of hearts, and the game is defeated if East is sufficiently alert to hop up with the spade ace and return a heart.

Oddly enough you would have no trouble on the more normal lead of a heart, for you would have been forced to rely on the spade suit for three tricks.

PROBLEM 2

♠ 5
♡ A 3
♢ Q 8 6 5 3
♣ Q 10 8 7 2

♠ A J
♡ Q 9 6 4
Game all.   ♢ A K
Dealer South.   ♣ K J 9 4 3

The Bidding

SOUTH	WEST	NORTH	EAST
1 ♣	Pass	3 ♣	Pass
3 ♡	Pass	5 ♣	Pass
6 ♣	Pass	Pass	Pass

The Lead

West leads the king of spades to your ace. How do you plan the play?

Review

Prospects are not too bright. You will be able to discard three heart losers from your hand only if the diamonds break 3–3. Can you give yourself an extra chance?

Solution

There is one slim possibility. A defender with short diamonds may have the bare ace of clubs and the king of hearts. You can gain a small advantage by playing on elimination lines and testing the diamonds before touching trumps.

Cash the ace and king of diamonds, ruff the jack of spades in dummy and continue with the diamond queen, throwing a heart from hand. If both defenders follow, you can knock out the ace of clubs, draw trumps and claim. And if someone uses the bare ace of trumps to ruff the diamond queen, he will have to return a heart or concede a ruff and discard. If the defender refuses to ruff, you simply ruff the fourth diamond yourself and throw him in with the trump.

The complete deal:

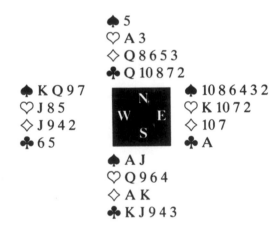

```
                 ♠ 5
                 ♡ A 3
                 ◇ Q 8 6 5 3
                 ♣ Q 10 8 7 2
♠ K Q 9 7                        ♠ 10 8 6 4 3 2
♡ J 8 5          N               ♡ K 10 7 2
◇ J 9 4 2     W     E            ◇ 10 7
♣ 6 5            S               ♣ A
                 ♠ A J
                 ♡ Q 9 6 4
                 ◇ A K
                 ♣ K J 9 4 3
```

Instead of playing the queen of diamonds at trick five you can just exit with a trump. It comes to the same thing, and East has to yield your twelfth trick in one way or another.

PROBLEM 3

♠ J 7 3 2
♡ 6 5
♢ 10 5 4 3
♣ Q 9 2

♠ K 5
♡ A J 10 7 4 2
♢ A Q
♣ A K 8

Game all.
Dealer West.

The Bidding

WEST	NORTH	EAST	SOUTH
1 ♢	Pass	Pass	2 ♢
Pass	2 ♠	Pass	4 ♡
Pass	Pass	Pass	

The Lead

West leads the ten of clubs. How do you plan the play?

Review

This does not look promising. There are two potential losers in spades, one in diamonds and at least one in hearts. How do you propose to play the trumps for one loser?

Solution

There are several options. You could win the first trick in dummy and lead a trump for a finesse. This will hold your loss to one trick when East has a doubleton honour or K Q x. On the bidding West will surely have at least one of the honours, however, and he is also more likely to have the doubleton. The play of the heart ace on the first round would cater for K Q doubleton, but it is far more likely that West will have K x or Q x.

The best plan is to win the first trick with the ace or king of clubs and lead the jack of hearts from hand. If West wins and returns a club, you can win in dummy and play another heart for a finesse. Once you have picked up the trumps, you should be able to produce a tenth trick in spades or diamonds by means of an end-play.

The complete deal:

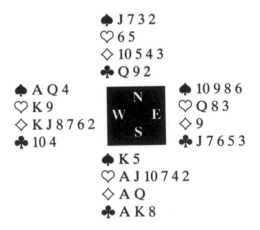

                ♠ J 7 3 2
                ♡ 6 5
                ♢ 10 5 4 3
                ♣ Q 9 2

♠ A Q 4   ♠ 10 9 8 6
♡ K 9   ♡ Q 8 3
♢ K J 8 7 6 2   ♢ 9
♣ 10 4   ♣ J 7 6 5 3

                ♠ K 5
                ♡ A J 10 7 4 2
                ♢ A Q
                ♣ A K 8

The defenders are helpless on the lie of the cards. If East wins the first trump and returns a spade, he sets up your tenth trick. If he returns his singleton diamond, you win with the ace, cash the ace and ten of hearts, play off the other top club in your hand and exit in diamonds. West, on lead, must yield your tenth trick in one suit or the other.

PROBLEM 4

♠ 6 5
♡ K Q 10 8 4
◇ 10 5
♣ A 9 6 3

♠ A 10 9 7 4 2
♡ 5

Love all.   ◇ Q 9 4 3
Dealer West.   ♣ J 4

The Bidding

WEST	NORTH	EAST	SOUTH
1 ♣	Pass	1 ♡	1 ♠
1 NT*	Pass	3 NT	Pass
Pass	Pass		

* *15–16*

The Lead

North leads the eight of spades. How are you going to defeat this game?

Review

The lead marks declarer with the three missing spade honours, and your lack of entries means that you have to abandon hope of establishing the suit. What else is there?

Solution

The only possible source of nourishment for the defence is the diamond suit. It must be correct to take your ace of spades at trick one and switch to a diamond.

There remains the question of which card to lead. Partner will need to have length in diamonds to give the defence a chance. One favourable possibility is that he has four diamonds headed by the king and jack plus the ace of hearts. If that is the position it will not matter which diamond you lead.

Alternatively partner may have four diamonds headed by the ace and jack, with perhaps the queen of clubs on the side. To cater for this possibility as well as the first one, you must switch to the queen of diamonds at trick two.

The complete deal:

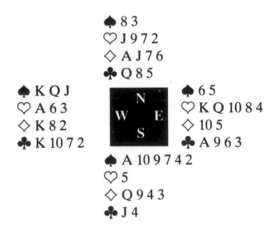

```
                    ♠ 8 3
                    ♡ J 9 7 2
                    ◇ A J 7 6
                    ♣ Q 8 5
    ♠ K Q J                      ♠ 6 5
    ♡ A 6 3          N           ♡ K Q 10 8 4
    ◇ K 8 2      W       E       ◇ 10 5
    ♣ K 10 7 2       S           ♣ A 9 6 3
                    ♠ A 10 9 7 4 2
                    ♡ 5
                    ◇ Q 9 4 3
                    ♣ J 4
```

As you can see, the lead of the queen of diamonds enables you to roll up the suit and take the first five tricks.

PROBLEM 5

♠ A Q J
♡ 5
♢ Q 7 6 2
♣ J 10 9 6 3

♠ K 9 7 5 4 3
♡ A K 10 6 4
♢ –
♣ A 5

Game all.
Dealer South.

The Bidding

SOUTH	WEST	NORTH	EAST
1 ♠	2 ♢	3 ♠	Pass
6 ♠	Pass	Pass	Pass

The Lead

West leads the ace of diamonds. East follows with the five and you ruff with the three of spades. How do you plan the play?

Review

The obvious plan is to establish the heart suit with two ruffs in dummy. For this to succeed you will need to find the hearts 4–3 and the spades 2–2. If the spades are 3–1 the singleton would need to be the ten. Is there anything better?

Solution

West's vulnerable overcall in diamonds suggest that you are unlikely to find even breaks in both majors. It must be better to play on cross-ruff lines and hope to finish with a throw-in and trump end-play.

Cash the top hearts, taking care to discard a club, not a diamond, from dummy. Ruff a heart with the jack of spades, ruff a diamond in hand, cash the ace of clubs and ruff another heart with the queen of spades. Three more ruffs in the red suits leave you in hand. Now you exit with the losing club and hope to score the king and nine of spades in the ending.

The complete deal:

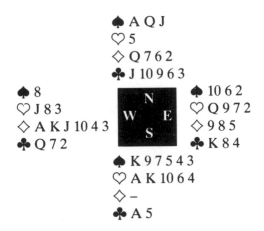

An initial trump lead would have defeated the slam by making it impossible for you to reduce your trumps sufficiently. A double-dummy lead of the jack of hearts would have had the same effect.

PROBLEM 6

♠ 8 3
♡ A 7 4 2
♢ A 10 8 6 4
♣ J 7

♠ A K Q 10 9 4
♡ J
♢ 5 3 2
♣ A 4 3

N–S game.
Dealer East.

The Bidding

WEST	NORTH	EAST	SOUTH
		Pass	1 ♠
Pass	2 ♢	Pass	3 ♠
Pass	4 ♠	Pass	Pass
Pass			

The Lead

West leads the five of hearts to dummy's ace. How do you plan the play?

Review

It looks like ten easy tricks – six trumps in your own hand, three side aces and a club ruff in dummy. Just about the only thing that can upset your plans is a bad trump break, in which case you might find yourself losing a trump trick as well as two diamonds and a club.

Solution

On this type of hand the best way of avoiding four losers is to cash your ten winners first. The key move is to ruff a heart at trick two. Then you can play a low club to the jack, win the trump return, cash the ace of clubs, ruff a club and ruff another heart.

The play of the top spades will reveal the trump position, and all will not be lost even if West has the guarded jack. You can still cross to dummy with the ace of diamonds and hope to ruff the fourth heart with the ten of trumps.

The complete deal:

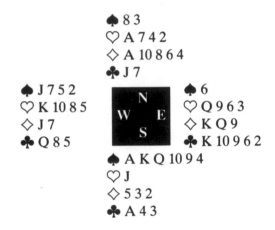

♠ 8 3
♡ A 7 4 2
◇ A 10 8 6 4
♣ J 7

♠ J 7 5 2
♡ K 10 8 5
◇ J 7
♣ Q 8 5

♠ 6
♡ Q 9 6 3
◇ K Q 9
♣ K 10 9 6 2

♠ A K Q 10 9 4
♡ J
◇ 5 3 2
♣ A 4 3

The contract is cold on a heart lead, but an initial lead of the jack of diamonds would have defeated you by leaving dummy an entry short for the trump-reducing play.

PROBLEM 7

♠ K 6 3
♡ J 7 6 3
♢ A K Q 5
♣ 9 4

♠ A 10 8 7 5 2
♡ A K
♢ J 7
♣ 10 7 6

E–W game.
Dealer West.

The Bidding

WEST	NORTH	EAST	SOUTH
Pass	1 NT	Pass	4 ♠
Pass	Pass	Pass	

The Lead

West leads the king of clubs and continues with the queen. East overtakes with the ace and plays a third club, and you ruff West's jack with dummy's three of spades. How should you continue?

Review

The problem here is to avoid the loss of two trump tricks in the event of a bad break. There is nothing to be done if West has all four trumps. Can you handle four trumps in the East hand?

Solution

If dummy's trumps had not been forced you would have had little difficulty in coping with four trumps in the East hand. Now the situation is different. You will be poorly placed if you cash the king of spades and West shows out. East will certainly split his honours on the next round, and you will have no way of preventing him from scoring two trump tricks.

What is needed is an extra entry in dummy to enable you to bring off a trump coup if the dangerous situation exists. That extra entry can be found by leaving the king of spades on the table. Lead the spade six and insert the ten if East plays low. West will be able to do no damage if he wins the trick.

If East plays an honour to force your ace and West shows out, you can cash the top hearts, play a diamond to dummy, ruff a heart, return in diamonds, and ruff another heart or a diamond. A trump to the king will then put you in a position to score your tenth trick *en passant* with the ten of spades.

The complete deal:

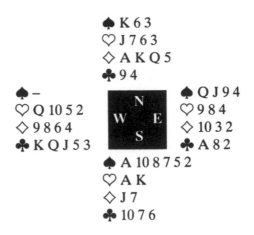

♠ K 6 3
♥ J 7 6 3
♦ A K Q 5
♣ 9 4

♠ –
♥ Q 10 5 2
♦ 9 8 6 4
♣ K Q J 5 3

♠ Q J 9 4
♥ 9 8 4
♦ 10 3 2
♣ A 8 2

♠ A 10 8 7 5 2
♥ A K
♦ J 7
♣ 10 7 6

PROBLEM 8

♠ A K 5
♡ A Q 9 4
◇ 6 2
♣ J 10 9 5

♠ J 2
♡ 6 5

Love all.
Dealer West.

◇ A Q J 10 7
♣ 8 7 6 3

The Bidding

WEST	NORTH	EAST	SOUTH
Pass	Pass	1 ♣	1 ◇
1 ♡	2 ◇	2 ♡	Pass
4 ♡	Pass	Pass	Pass

The Lead

North leads the nine of diamonds to your ace, West following with the three. How should you continue?

Review

The opening lead marks the king of diamonds in the West hand. You can hardly expect a trump trick for the defence, and it looks as though you need three tricks in the black suits. Will that be possible?

Solution

Partner will need to score a spade trick as well as a couple of clubs if the contract is to be defeated. This is not the moment for a passive trump or diamond return. The spades must be attacked immediately before discards become available on dummy's clubs.

The orthodox lead from a doubleton holding is the top card, but that may not be good enough here. You will never be on lead again, and if you waste the power of the jack of spades partner may not be able to continue the attack when he later gains the lead in clubs. You have to cater for the possibility of partner having the queen and nine of spades, not just the queen and ten, and the way to do that is by switching to the two of spades at trick two.

The complete deal:

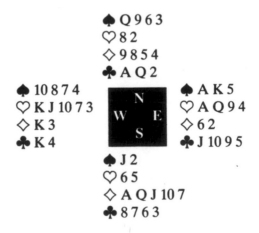

```
              ♠ Q 9 6 3
              ♡ 8 2
              ◇ 9 8 5 4
              ♣ A Q 2
♠ 10 8 7 4                    ♠ A K 5
♡ K J 10 7 3       N          ♡ A Q 9 4
◇ K 3          W       E      ◇ 6 2
♣ K 4              S          ♣ J 10 9 5
              ♠ J 2
              ♡ 6 5
              ◇ A Q J 10 7
              ♣ 8 7 6 3
```

By preserving the jack of spades you make it safe for partner to return a small spade when he wins the first round of clubs, thus establishing a fourth trick for the defence.

PROBLEM 9

♠ 8 7 4 3
♡ 9
♢ J 10 4 2
♣ J 8 5 4

♠ A J 10 9 2
♡ A K 5
♢ A Q 8 7 3
♣ –

N–S game.
Dealer East.

The Bidding

WEST	NORTH	EAST	SOUTH
		1 ♡*	1 ♠
3 ♡	Pass	4 ♡	5 ♢
Pass	Pass	Dble	Pass
Pass	5 ♠	Pass	Pass
Dble	Pass	Pass	Pass

5-card major

The Lead

West leads the jack of hearts to your ace. How do you plan the play?

Review

The bidding suggests that the diamond finesse will be right but that the spade honours will be offside. The dangerous case is where West has all four missing trumps. Can you overcome this hazard?

Solution

You are lucky to have escaped an initial club lead, but you can be sure that you will be forced in clubs each time West regains the lead. This means that you cannot afford to test the position by cashing the spade ace, for if West has four trumps he will end up making three of them. Instead you must use your intermediate trumps to knock out West's honours.

Play the jack of spades at trick two, ruff the club return with the nine, and continue with the ten of spades. You can ruff the next club with the spade ace and draw the remaining trumps with the eight and seven in dummy. A diamond finesse will then bring in the rest of the tricks.

The complete deal:

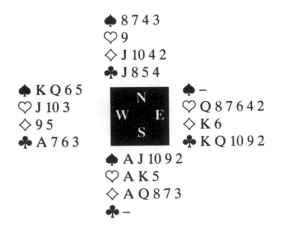

```
              ♠ 8 7 4 3
              ♡ 9
              ◇ J 10 4 2
              ♣ J 8 5 4
♠ K Q 6 5                      ♠ —
♡ J 10 3          N           ♡ Q 8 7 6 4 2
◇ 9 5         W       E       ◇ K 6
♣ A 7 6 3         S           ♣ K Q 10 9 2
              ♠ A J 10 9 2
              ♡ A K 5
              ◇ A Q 8 7 3
              ♣ —
```

Perhaps North should have passed the double of five diamonds. This contract is easily made even if West starts with a low spade for his partner to ruff.

PROBLEM 10

♠ A 5 3
♡ A Q 10 7
♢ 9 6 5
♣ J 10 8

♠ K Q J 10 8 7 4 2
♡ J 3
♢ K 7 4
♣ –

N–S game.
Dealer South.

The Bidding

SOUTH	WEST	NORTH	EAST
4 ♠	Pass	Pass	Pass

The Lead

West leads the ace of clubs and partner puts down a pleasing dummy. How do you plan the play?

Review

You have nine top tricks and excellent prospects of an extra trick or two in the red suits. The only danger is that you might lose one heart and three diamonds. Can you avoid all risk?

Solution

You need to find a way of developing a second heart trick without allowing East to gain the lead. Once you direct your mind to the problem the solution is not too hard to see.

Just allow West to win the first trick with the ace of clubs, discarding a heart from your hand. You can win a heart switch with the ace, draw two rounds of trumps with the king and ace and then run the queen of hearts, discarding a diamond unless East produces the king. Ten tricks are guaranteed, since you still have a trump entry in dummy to reach the established ten of hearts.

The complete deal:

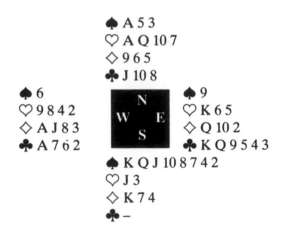

```
              ♠ A 5 3
              ♡ A Q 10 7
              ◇ 9 6 5
              ♣ J 10 8
  ♠ 6                          ♠ 9
  ♡ 9 8 4 2          N         ♡ K 6 5
  ◇ A J 8 3     W       E      ◇ Q 10 2
  ♣ A 7 6 2          S         ♣ K Q 9 5 4 3
              ♠ K Q J 10 8 7 4 2
              ♡ J 3
              ◇ K 7 4
              ♣ –
```

As you can see, any other line of play results in defeat on the lie of the cards.

PROBLEM 11

♠ K J 5
♡ 7 6 2
♢ A 8 6 3
♣ A Q 5

♠ Q 10 2
♡ K Q 4
♢ K Q 7
♣ J 7 4 3

Game all.
Dealer North.

The Bidding

WEST	NORTH	EAST	SOUTH
	1 ♢	1 ♡	3 NT
Pass	Pass	Pass	

The Lead

West leads the nine of hearts, East covers with the ten and you win with the king. What do you play at trick two?

Review

Nine tricks may not be easy in spite of your combined total of 27 high-card points. If the diamonds fail to break 3–3 you will need two tricks from clubs as well as two from spades.

Solution

If West has one of the key cards – the ace of spades or the king of clubs – the contract is safe provided that you tackle the suits in the right order. It would be a mistake to lead a spade at trick two, since West might win and lead another heart to let East clear the suit. A losing club finesse would then result in defeat.

Taking the club finesse first gives a better chance. If the finesse wins you can switch to spades, while if the finesse loses it may use up East's only entry for the long hearts.

However, it would be unwise to lead a club at trick two since East could have both the spade ace and the club king. To retain all your chances you should test the diamonds first. Play a diamond to the ace and then cash the king and queen. If the suit proves to be 3–3 you can make sure of nine tricks by switching to spades. If a defender shows out on the second or third round of diamonds, you can take your best remaining chance by finessing the queen of clubs.

The complete deal:

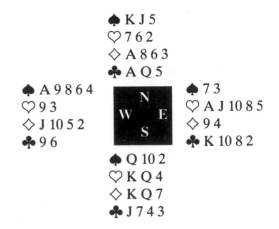

```
              ♠ K J 5
              ♡ 7 6 2
              ◇ A 8 6 3
              ♣ A Q 5
♠ A 9 8 6 4        N         ♠ 7 3
♡ 9 3          W       E     ♡ A J 10 8 5
◇ J 10 5 2         S         ◇ 9 4
♣ 9 6                        ♣ K 10 8 2
              ♠ Q 10 2
              ♡ K Q 4
              ◇ K Q 7
              ♣ J 7 4 3
```

PROBLEM 12

♠ Q 10 9 6
♡ A K Q 9 4
♢ 10 6 3
♣ 4

♠ K 7 5 4
♡ 6 5

Game all.   ♢ A K 8 2
Dealer West.   ♣ K 7 3

The Bidding

WEST	NORTH	EAST	SOUTH
1 ♡	Pass	2 ♣	Pass
2 ♡	Pass	2 ♠	Pass
3 ♠	Pass	5 ♣	Pass
Pass	Pass		

The Lead

On your lead of the ace of diamonds North plays the queen and East the five. What now?

Review

Partner's play of the queen of diamonds announces that it is safe for you to underlead on the second round. If you could put North in with the jack of diamonds, a spade return would defeat the contract by at least two tricks. But is this defence really safe?

Solution

The trouble is that there may not be a second diamond trick to cash. In any case you don't need it. On the assumption that declarer has no more than seven clubs, you can make sure of defeating this contract by switching to a heart at trick two.

East's failure to support hearts marks him with no more than two cards in the suit, and when you are in with the king of clubs you can complete the job of severing communications by leading your second heart. Declarer is prevented from enjoying more than two heart tricks, and the king of spades is bound to score the setting trick.

The complete deal:

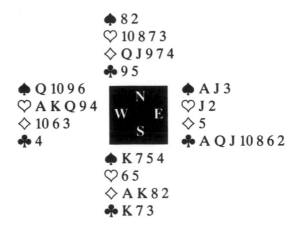

```
              ♠ 8 2
              ♡ 10 8 7 3
              ◇ Q J 9 7 4
              ♣ 9 5
  ♠ Q 10 9 6      N        ♠ A J 3
  ♡ A K Q 9 4   W   E      ♡ J 2
  ◇ 10 6 3        S        ◇ 5
  ♣ 4                      ♣ A Q J 10 8 6 2
              ♠ K 7 5 4
              ♡ 6 5
              ◇ A K 8 2
              ♣ K 7 3
```

Note that on a diamond continuation declarer can ruff, knock out the king of trumps, and eventually discard his losing spades on the hearts.

PROBLEM 13

♠ K 6
♡ 3
♢ Q 10 5 4
♣ A J 10 9 5 3

♠ Q 5
♡ A 9 5 4
♢ K J 9 6 3 2
♣ 7

Game all.
Dealer East.

The Bidding

WEST	NORTH	EAST	SOUTH
		1 ♣	2 ♢
3 ♠	5 ♢	Pass	Pass
Dble	Pass	Pass	Pass

The Lead

West attacks with the ace and another diamond, East discarding the two of spades on the second round. You win in hand, play a club to the ace and return a small club, ruffing out East's queen. How should you continue?

Review

You need to establish a club for a discard of your fourth heart. There will be no trouble if the clubs are 3–3, but West may have started with four clubs. What can you do about it?

[109]

Solution

If West has four clubs you will need three entries in dummy – two to establish the suit and one to reach the winning club. You can reach dummy twice by ruffing hearts but the third entry, which can only come from spades, must be established without delay.

East is likely to have the ace of spades, but this is not important. You should play the queen of spades from hand at trick five. If East takes his ace and returns the suit, you can ruff out the clubs in comfort.

East may deny you an entry in spades by playing low on the first round, but this will not help his cause. After the ace of hearts and a heart ruff you return the jack of clubs, discarding the remaining spade from your hand. West can win with the king of clubs but this is the last trick for the defence.

The complete deal:

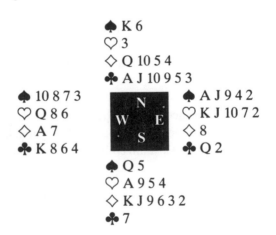

```
                    ♠ K 6
                    ♡ 3
                    ◇ Q 10 5 4
                    ♣ A J 10 9 5 3
      ♠ 10 8 7 3         N         ♠ A J 9 4 2
      ♡ Q 8 6                       ♡ K J 10 7 2
      ◇ A 7        W    E           ◇ 8
      ♣ K 8 6 4         S           ♣ Q 2
                    ♠ Q 5
                    ♡ A 9 5 4
                    ◇ K J 9 6 3 2
                    ♣ 7
```

PROBLEM 14

♠ 6 4
♡ A 3
◇ Q J 8 5 4
♣ A 7 4 2

E–W game.
Dealer South.

♠ A Q J
♡ K Q 8 6 5 4 2
◇ A 9 2
♣ –

The Bidding

SOUTH	WEST	NORTH	EAST
1 ♡	Pass	2 ◇	Pass
4 ♡	Pass	5 ♣	Pass
5 ◇	Pass	5 ♡	Pass
6 ♡	Pass	Pass	Pass

The Lead

West leads the jack of clubs. How do you plan the play?

Review

There are chances of developing the extra tricks you need in either diamonds or spades. One obvious trap to avoid is playing the ace of clubs at trick one, for you do not know at this stage what you want to discard.

Solution

Ruff the first trick and test the trumps with the king and ace. On a 2–2 break you can make a near certainty of the slam by continuing with the queen of diamonds. If East covers with the king, you win with the ace, return to the diamond jack, discard your third diamond on the club ace and, if the diamond ten has not dropped, switch to spades. If East plays low on the queen of diamonds (or if he shows out), you should unblock the nine from your hand. If the queen holds, again you discard your losing diamond on the club ace and turn to the spades.

If West wins with the king of diamonds, you will always be able to score three diamond tricks except when the king is singleton. Even then you have the chance of the spade finesse.

On a 3–1 trump break you cannot afford the luxury of playing the diamonds like this. Instead you should ruff another club, draw the last trump, cash the ace of diamonds and continue with a diamond to the queen. You will make the slam unless West has a small singleton or void in diamonds and the king of spades.

The complete deal:

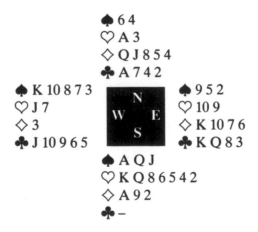

♠ 6 4
♥ A 3
♦ Q J 8 5 4
♣ A 7 4 2

♠ K 10 8 7 3   ♠ 9 5 2
♥ J 7   ♥ 10 9
♦ 3   ♦ K 10 7 6
♣ J 10 9 6 5   ♣ K Q 8 3

♠ A Q J
♥ K Q 8 6 5 4 2
♦ A 9 2
♣ –

PROBLEM 15

♠ 6 2
♡ A K 6 5
♢ A K Q J
♣ 9 4 3

♠ K 8 4
♡ 10 8 7 3 2
♢ 7 4
♣ K Q 7

N–S game.
Dealer West.

The Bidding

WEST	NORTH	EAST	SOUTH
1 NT*	Dble	2 ♠	2 NT
Pass	3 ♢	Pass	3 ♡
Pass	4 ♡	Pass	Pass
Pass			

*13–15

The Lead

West leads the ten of diamonds to dummy's jack. How do you plan the play?

Review

There will be no trouble if the trumps break 2–2, but on the bidding West is likely to have a trump stopper. Can you handle this?

Solution

It would be dangerous to test the trumps too soon. West is marked with most of the high cards, and you must plan to throw him in with the third trump at a time when he must either open up the spades or give you a ruff and discard. That involves eliminating the minors, and the correct move at trick two is to play a club to your king.

If West takes his ace you can win any return, unblock the queen of clubs, draw one round of trumps, discard your third club on a diamond and ruff a club in hand. A trump to dummy is followed by the fourth diamond, and West is ripe for the trump throw-in.

If West refuses to win the ace of clubs, you simply draw a couple of rounds of trumps and then discard your remaining clubs on the diamonds.

The complete deal:

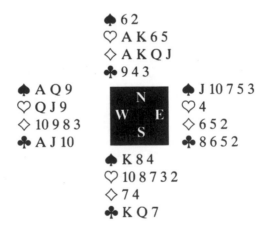

Note that it is hazardous to draw even one round of trumps before playing on clubs. If West returns a trump after winning the ace of clubs, you will be reduced to guessing whether he started with three or four diamonds.

PROBLEM 16

```
        ♠ 9 4
        ♡ A 7          ┌─────────┐
        ◇ 8 7 6 3 2    │    N    │
        ♣ K 8 6 4      │ W     E │
                       │    S    │
                       └─────────┘
                       ♠ Q 8 5
                       ♡ K 4 3
Game all.              ◇ K 10 9
Dealer East.           ♣ Q 10 9 7
```

The Bidding

WEST	NORTH	EAST	SOUTH
		2 NT	Pass
3 NT	Pass	Pass	Pass

The Lead

You lead the ten of clubs and the trick is won by the king, North playing the two and East the three. Next comes the two of diamonds to the jack, queen and king. Plan your defence.

Review

Partner can have very little in the way of high cards in the light of East's strong opening bid. Is there any hope for the defence?

Solution

Declarer appears to have the ace and another diamond left in his hand, and he is sure to make his contract if he is allowed to score the long diamonds on the table. The clubs must therefore wait while you attend to the more urgent business of attacking the entry in dummy.

It is no good leading a small heart in the hope of finding partner with the queen. Partner is marked with the jacks in the minor suits: if he has the queen of hearts as well, East does not have his twenty points. At trick three you must play the king of hearts to make sure of knocking out dummy's ace. This is likely to give declarer an extra heart trick, but by denying him diamond tricks it may bring about the defeat of the game.

The complete deal:

```
              ♠ J 10 3 2
              ♡ 10 9 8 5
              ◇ J 4
              ♣ J 5 2
  ♠ 9 4                        ♠ A K 7 6
  ♡ A 7                        ♡ Q J 6 2
  ◇ 8 7 6 3 2                  ◇ A Q 5
  ♣ K 8 6 4                    ♣ A 3
              ♠ Q 8 5
              ♡ K 4 3
              ◇ K 10 9
              ♣ Q 10 9 7
```

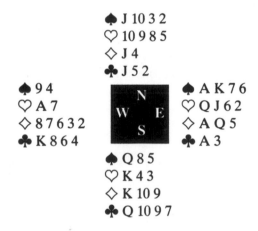

Declarer could have succeeded by winning in hand at trick one and playing a low diamond. On winning the second club he can continue with the ace and queen of diamonds. Four tricks are established for the defence, but the declarer makes the rest with the help of the heart finesse.

PROBLEM 17

♠ A K 6 3
♡ Q 5 2
♢ 8 6 4 2
♣ Q 7

```
      N
  W       E
      S
```

♠ 10 2
♡ A K J 10 4
♢ A
♣ K J 10 9 2

Game all.
Dealer South.

The Bidding

SOUTH	WEST	NORTH	EAST
1 ♡	Pass	1 ♠	Pass
3 ♣	Pass	5 ♡	Pass
6 ♡	Pass	Pass	Pass

The Lead

West leads the queen of diamonds to your ace. You cash the ace of hearts and receive a shock when East discards a diamond. Both opponents follow small when you play the two of clubs to dummy's queen. How should you continue?

Review

Obviously you must knock out the ace of clubs before playing any more trumps. Do you foresee any snags?

Solution

When you knock out the ace of clubs a diamond is sure to come back, leaving you with one trump fewer than West. Your plan must be to use the clubs as substitute trumps, running them until West ruffs. As soon as he ruffs in, you can over-ruff on the table and draw trumps for twelve tricks.

The trouble is that West may not co-operate with this plan. Instead of ruffing a club he may discard all his spades and eventually score a spade ruff as the setting trick. To guard against this possibility you should cash one top spade before playing a second club. Then, if West refuses to ruff clubs, you can discard all the remaining spades from dummy and finish with a spade ruff.

The complete deal:

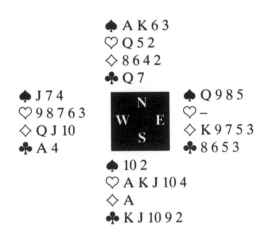

```
              ♠ A K 6 3
              ♡ Q 5 2
              ◇ 8 6 4 2
              ♣ Q 7
♠ J 7 4                        ♠ Q 9 8 5
♡ 9 8 7 6 3       N            ♡ –
◇ Q J 10      W       E        ◇ K 9 7 5 3
♣ A 4             S            ♣ 8 6 5 3
              ♠ 10 2
              ♡ A K J 10 4
              ◇ A
              ♣ K J 10 9 2
```

PROBLEM 18

♠ Q 5 4 3
♡ Q J 3 2
◇ K J 10 6
♣ 7

♠ A 9 8 7 6
♡ A 10 4
◇ A 9 8
♣ 8 3

Game all.
Dealer South.

The Bidding

SOUTH	WEST	NORTH	EAST
1 ♠	2 ♣	3 ♠	3 NT
Pass	Pass	4 ♠	Dble
Pass	Pass	Pass	

The Lead

West leads the four of diamonds to the jack, queen and ace. How do you continue?

Review

East must surely have all the outstanding trumps to justify his double, so you have two certain trump losers as well as a loser in clubs. Assuming the heart finesse to be right, as seems probable on the bidding, are you in any danger of losing a fourth trick?

Solution

The only danger is that East may be able to score a third trump trick by ruffing before you can extract all his trumps. If East started with a doubleton diamond, for instance, it will not do to concede a trump trick to him immediately. He will return his diamond, win the third round of trumps, put his partner in with a club, and score a diamond ruff to defeat the contract.

There is a simple way of neutralizing this threat. Just lead a club at trick two to put the defenders out of touch with each other.

The complete deal:

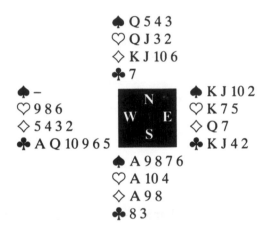

♠ Q 5 4 3
♥ Q J 3 2
♦ K J 10 6
♣ 7

♠ –
♥ 9 8 6
♦ 5 4 3 2
♣ A Q 10 9 6 5

♠ K J 10 2
♥ K 7 5
♦ Q 7
♣ K J 4 2

♠ A 9 8 7 6
♥ A 10 4
♦ A 9 8
♣ 8 3

The club lead at trick two restricts the defenders to three tricks – one club and two spades.

PROBLEM 19

♠ Q 5
♡ A K J 10 6 2
◇ Q 6 5 2
♣ 4

♠ K J 6 4 2
♡ 9 5
N–S game. ◇ J 7 3
Dealer East. ♣ A J 7

The Bidding

WEST	NORTH	EAST	SOUTH
		3 ♣	Pass
Pass	3 ♡	Pass	3 NT
Pass	Pass	Pass	

The Lead

West leads the eight of clubs to the queen and ace. You play a spade to the queen and return a spade to the jack and ace, East echoing with the eight and the three. West surprises you by switching to the queen of hearts, and East follows with the seven when you play dummy's ace. Take it from there.

Review

West is clearly trying to jam your communications, having realised that the king of spades will be your ninth trick if you can reach it. You have to look for a way of foiling this plan.

Solution

It would not be sensible to run the heart suit immediately, for that would prepare the way for a black-suit squeeze against yourself. Suppose that you discarded two spades and two diamonds on the hearts and then led a diamond. West would win and cash his other top diamond (on the bidding he is pretty sure to have them both), and you would have to make an impossible choice between throwing the king of spades and unguarding the clubs.

Since you have an entry in the nine of hearts, it must be perfectly safe to lead a diamond to your jack at trick five. You can win the heart return with the nine, temporarily cutting yourself adrift from dummy. A further diamond lead will re-establish contact and assure you of nine tricks.

The complete deal:

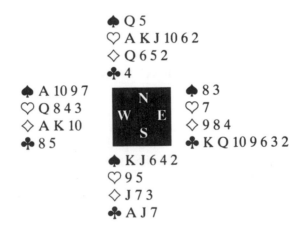

```
                  ♠ Q 5
                  ♡ A K J 10 6 2
                  ◇ Q 6 5 2
                  ♣ 4
  ♠ A 10 9 7                        ♠ 8 3
  ♡ Q 8 4 3         N              ♡ 7
  ◇ A K 10       W     E           ◇ 9 8 4
  ♣ 8 5             S              ♣ K Q 10 9 6 3 2
                  ♠ K J 6 4 2
                  ♡ 9 5
                  ◇ J 7 3
                  ♣ A J 7
```

PROBLEM 20

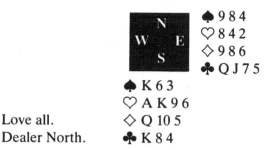

♠ 9 8 4
♡ 8 4 2
◇ 9 8 6
♣ Q J 7 5

♠ K 6 3
♡ A K 9 6

Love all.
Dealer North.

◇ Q 10 5
♣ K 8 4

The Bidding

WEST	NORTH	EAST	SOUTH
	Pass	Pass	1 ♡
Dble	2 ♡	Pass	Pass
3 ♠	Pass	4 ♠	Pass
Pass	Pass		

The Lead

North leads the queen of hearts and continues with the five of hearts to your king, West following with the three and the seven. How do you continue?

Review

East has little enough for his raise to game, and partner cannot have much apart from his heart honours. You can place declarer with a semi-solid six-card spade suit and the top cards in the minor suits. You may hope for a third defensive trick in diamonds, but what about the fourth?

Solution

Although your black kings are poorly placed, it is not going to be easy for declarer to reach dummy in order to take his finesses.

The simple defence is to continue with a third heart, but this is not as safe as it seems. You may be subjected to a subsequent throw-in and compelled to give the lead to dummy. The exit card in hearts must be retained for use in the later stages. Since you need a diamond trick anyway if the contract is to be defeated, it must be right to switch to diamonds at trick three.

The complete deal:

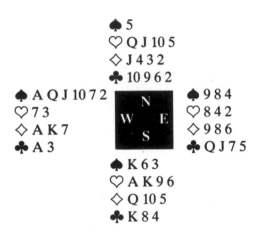

You see what happens if you continue hearts at trick three? Declarer ruffs and plays three rounds of diamonds, and the defender who wins the trick cannot avoid letting dummy in to take the finesses in the black suits.

PROBLEM 21

♠ A Q 2
♡ 8 5
♢ K 8 6 5
♣ A 9 5 3

♠ K J 10 7 6 4
♡ K 3
♢ A Q 7 3
♣ 4

Game all.
Dealer East.

The Bidding

WEST	NORTH	EAST	SOUTH
		1 ♡	2 ♠
Pass	3 ♡	Pass	3 ♠
Pass	4 ♣	Pass	4 ♢
Pass	5 ♠	Pass	6 ♠
Pass	Pass	Pass	

The Lead

West leads the nine of diamonds. How do you plan the play?

Review

With the ace of hearts marked in the East hand it looks as though a heart should be your only loser. But West must have a powerful reason for rejecting the lead of his partner's suit, which may well mean that the diamond nine is a singleton. Can you cope with this?

Solution

You must win the first trick in dummy in order to have a chance of picking up the diamonds, and you will have to draw trumps before messing around in the side suits. This will lead to entry problems if the trumps are 3–1. You need to finesse twice in diamonds and lead a heart towards your king, and you have to accomplish this with only two entries in dummy.

A far-sighted unblocking play is required. You should win the first trick with the king of diamonds and drop the seven from your hand. Draw trumps, playing three rounds if necessary, and then lead the eight of diamonds from dummy. East does best to cover, but you win with the queen, return to the ace of clubs, and continue with the six of diamonds. It makes no difference whether East covers or not. If he plays low, the lead remains on the table for a heart towards your king. If East covers the six of diamonds, you win with the ace and return to the diamond five for the heart lead.

The complete deal:

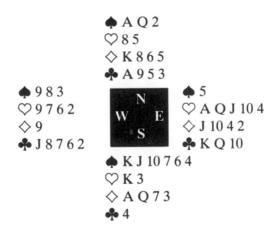

```
              ♠ A Q 2
              ♡ 8 5
              ◇ K 8 6 5
              ♣ A 9 5 3
♠ 9 8 3                      ♠ 5
♡ 9 7 6 2        N          ♡ A Q J 10 4
◇ 9          W       E      ◇ J 10 4 2
♣ J 8 7 6 2      S          ♣ K Q 10
              ♠ K J 10 7 6 4
              ♡ K 3
              ◇ A Q 7 3
              ♣ 4
```

Defenders are often tempted to lead singletons against slams. Sometimes it works, but more often it is better to lead partner's suit. Your slam would have had no chance after a heart to the ace and a club switch.

PROBLEM 22

♠ K 10 9 3
♡ –
♢ A K J 9 6 5 3
♣ A 8

♠ A Q J 8
♡ K 8 7 5
Game all.   ♢ 4
Dealer South.   ♣ Q J 6 3

The Bidding

SOUTH	WEST	NORTH	EAST
1 ♣	Pass	3 ♢	Pass
3 ♡	Pass	3 ♠	Pass
4 ♣	Pass	6 ♠	Pass
Pass	Pass		

The Lead

West leads the jack of hearts. How do you plan the play?

Review

If everything breaks evenly and the king of clubs is well placed it may be possible to make all thirteen tricks. Your task, however, is to find the safest way of making twelve tricks.

Solution

You will need to ruff diamonds in your hand, and if the trumps are 4–1 you cannot afford to allow dummy to be forced. You should therefore discard on the jack of hearts and allow East to win the first trick.

There is still room for carelessness. It looks natural to discard the eight of clubs from the table, but if you do this East is sure to return a club at trick two. The removal of the club entry may be fatal. If both spades and diamonds prove to be 4–1, you will be short of an entry to establish the diamonds and the slam will go one down.

The correct discard from dummy at trick one is a small diamond. The king of hearts will take care of the losing club at a later stage. Now if East switches to a club you can expect to make two club tricks. You can count on one trick in each of the red suits, and a cross-ruff should bring the tally up to twelve.

The complete deal:

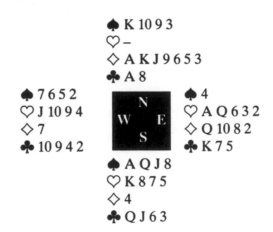

```
                ♠ K 10 9 3
                ♡ –
                ◇ A K J 9 6 5 3
                ♣ A 8
  ♠ 7 6 5 2                      ♠ 4
  ♡ J 10 9 4          N          ♡ A Q 6 3 2
  ◇ 7            W         E      ◇ Q 10 8 2
  ♣ 10 9 4 2          S          ♣ K 7 5
                ♠ A Q J 8
                ♡ K 8 7 5
                ◇ 4
                ♣ Q J 6 3
```

PROBLEM 23

♠ Q 5
♡ Q 7 2
♢ K 9 8 5
♣ K 10 6 3

♠ A K 10 8 7 4 2
♡ 8
♢ A 10 6
♣ 9 5

N–S game.
Dealer West.

The Bidding

WEST	NORTH	EAST	SOUTH
Pass	Pass	1 ♡	2 ♠
Pass	3 ♠	Pass	4 ♠
Pass	Pass	Pass	

The Lead

West leads the three of diamonds to the five, jack and ace. You draw trumps in three rounds, throwing a club from dummy while East discards two hearts. How should you continue?

Review

There are nine top tricks, and at first glance it seems a simple matter to establish a tenth in diamonds. Could anything go wrong?

Solution

Running the ten of diamonds will bring in an overtrick if the initial lead was from the queen, but you have no guarantee that this is the case. The three of diamonds may be a singleton or the top card of a doubleton. On winning his diamond trick, East might be able to put his partner on lead with a heart, and a club switch could set up four tricks for the defence.

To give yourself every chance at this point you must cut the defensive communications by leading a heart. If East wins the trick, you will subsequently be able to run the diamond ten with complete safety.

If West is able to win the heart trick, the contract will still be safe even if East has all three club honours. On a heart or diamond return you can again duck a diamond to East. And on a club return you can play low from dummy, hoping to set up a club trick or to end-play East in the minors.

The complete deal:

♠ Q 5
♥ Q 7 2
♦ K 9 8 5
♣ K 10 6 3

♠ J 9 3
♥ K 9 6 4
♦ 3 2
♣ J 7 4 2

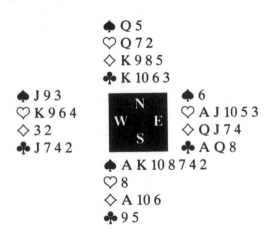

♠ 6
♥ A J 10 5 3
♦ Q J 7 4
♣ A Q 8

♠ A K 10 8 7 4 2
♥ 8
♦ A 10 6
♣ 9 5

PROBLEM 24

♠ J 7 6 4
♡ 8 5
◇ A Q 10
♣ K 9 8 3

♠ K Q 10
♡ A 9 7 4 2

E–W game.   ◇ 9 4
Dealer West.   ♣ J 5 2

The Bidding

WEST	NORTH	EAST	SOUTH
1 ♠	Pass	3 ♠	Pass
4 ♠	Pass	Pass	Pass

The Lead

North leads the queen of hearts and West plays the six under your ace. On the heart return declarer plays the king and partner the three. Declarer runs the jack of diamonds and continues with a diamond to the queen, partner following low-high. Then comes a spade to the ten and ace, North playing the three, and a diamond to dummy's ace. How do you plan the defence?

Review

Declarer does not have much in high-card strength for his bid of four spades and is sure to have five trumps. You have one heart and two trump tricks, and to defeat the contract you must also make a trick in clubs. Any ideas?

Solution

Declarer is marked with five spades, two hearts, three diamonds and therefore three clubs, and you will always make a club trick if North has Q 10 x in the suit. But West may have the club ten. He seems to be angling for an elimination, hoping to cash three diamonds before throwing you in with a trump.

Refusing to ruff the diamond will merely postpone your fate. And if you ruff, cash the master trump and lead a club, declarer is likely to do the right thing by playing for dividend honours in clubs.

There is just one manoeuvre worth trying. You should ruff the ace of diamonds and switch immediately to the jack of clubs without cashing your master trump. It may then appear to declarer that the trumps were 2–2 all the time, in which case he has a cinch for his contract by capturing the club jack in dummy with the king and playing a trump to end-play North. Great will be West's dismay when you produce the trump and play another club.

The complete deal:

```
                ♠ 3
                ♡ Q J 10 3
                ◇ K 7 6 5 2
                ♣ Q 7 4
  ♠ A 9 8 5 2                    ♠ J 7 6 4
  ♡ K 6            N             ♡ 8 5
  ◇ J 8 3       W     E          ◇ A Q 10
  ♣ A 10 6         S             ♣ K 9 8 3
                ♠ K Q 10
                ♡ A 9 7 4 2
                ◇ 9 4
                ♣ J 5 2
```

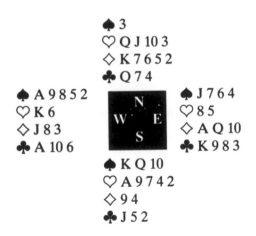

[132]

PROBLEM 25

♠ K J
♡ J 9 6 3
♢ –
♣ A J 9 8 7 4 2

♠ A 10 9 8 6 5 3
♡ Q 10
Game all.   ♢ 9 8 5 2
Dealer North.   ♣ –

The Bidding

WEST	NORTH	EAST	SOUTH
	1 ♣	1 NT	3 ♠
3 NT	4 ♠	Dble	Pass
Pass	Pass		

The Lead

West leads the ace of hearts on which East plays the two and you the queen. Next comes a switch to the two of spades, East playing the four under dummy's jack. How do you plan the play?

Review

The bidding indicates that East is likely to have the outstanding trumps. In that case you look like losing a trump trick if you ruff a diamond in dummy. You will have a chance of ten tricks if you are allowed to establish two hearts, of course. Are there any other possibilities?

[133]

Solution

It is highly unlikely that the opponents will let you establish two heart tricks. If you play a low heart from dummy at trick three, your ten will be allowed to win and you will be held to nine tricks.

To give yourself a chance you must assume that West has the heart king and that the clubs are 3–3. Cash the ace of clubs, discarding a diamond from hand, ruff a club and advance the ten of hearts. If West wins with the king and returns a diamond, you can ruff in dummy and force East to ruff the fourth heart at the cost of his trump trick. If West plays low on the ten of hearts, you overtake with the jack and ruff another club. Now, after a 3–3 club break, you are in a similar happy position. Ruff a diamond in dummy and continue with a winning club to pick up East's trumps.

The complete deal:

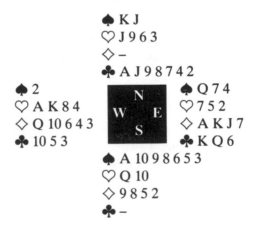

```
                    ♠ K J
                    ♡ J 9 6 3
                    ◇ –
                    ♣ A J 9 8 7 4 2
   ♠ 2              ┌─────────┐      ♠ Q 7 4
   ♡ A K 8 4        │    N    │      ♡ 7 5 2
   ◇ Q 10 6 4 3     │  W   E  │      ◇ A K J 7
   ♣ 10 5 3         │    S    │      ♣ K Q 6
                    └─────────┘
                    ♠ A 10 9 8 6 5 3
                    ♡ Q 10
                    ◇ 9 8 5 2
                    ♣ –
```

Note that three no-trumps is a make because of the blockage in spades. An initial trump lead, or even a diamond, would have defeated your spade game.

PROBLEM 26

♠ 9 6
♡ 8 6
♢ Q J 10 8 7
♣ K Q 7 4

♠ A K 10 5
♡ K Q 10 2
♢ A 9 4
♣ 9 5

Game all.
Dealer South.

The Bidding

SOUTH	WEST	NORTH	EAST
1 NT	Pass	2 NT	Pass
3 NT	Pass	Pass	Pass

The Lead

West leads the five of hearts to his partner's ace. After a little thought East returns the jack of clubs. West follows with the two and you win reluctantly with the queen. Dummy's entry has been removed before you were ready to use it. Now you must hope for a favourable diamond position. When you run the queen of diamonds both defenders play small. The same thing happens when you continue with the jack of diamonds. What now?

Review

You have eight top tricks and it looks as though you will have to rely on the spade suit for the ninth. One slim chance is to lead the small spade from dummy at this point, hoping for East to have both honours. Can you do better?

Solution

There is a good chance of making the contract not only when East has both spade honours but also when he has any four cards headed by the queen or the jack.

First you must remove some of the enemy exit cards. Continue with a diamond to the ace, cash one heart winner, and then lead the five of spades from hand. If West wins the trick he will have to play on clubs since a major-suit return gives you the contract. And your club nine may prevent the defenders from scoring more than two tricks in the suit. You discard the ten of hearts on the third round of clubs and East, if he has no heart left, will have to switch back to spades, giving you a finesse for the contract.

If it is East who wins the first spade he will have to return the suit. Now you just play the ace and king of spades and, if the remaining honour does not fall, continue with the fourth spade in the hope of end-playing East.

The complete deal:

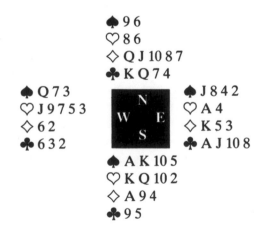

```
                    ♠ 9 6
                    ♡ 8 6
                    ◇ Q J 10 8 7
                    ♣ K Q 7 4
♠ Q 7 3                              ♠ J 8 4 2
♡ J 9 7 5 3         N                ♡ A 4
◇ 6 2           W       E            ◇ K 5 3
♣ 6 3 2             S                ♣ A J 10 8
                    ♠ A K 10 5
                    ♡ K Q 10 2
                    ◇ A 9 4
                    ♣ 9 5
```

PROBLEM 27

♠ 6 2
♡ K J 7 6
♢ 10
♣ A K 8 6 5 3

♠ K Q J 7 5
♡ A 10 8 3
♢ 9
♣ J 7 4

E–W game.
Dealer North.

The Bidding

WEST	NORTH	EAST	SOUTH
	1 ♣	2 ♢*	2 ♠
3 ♢	Pass	Pass	3 ♡
Pass	4 ♡	Pass	Pass
Pass			

* *Intermediate*

The Lead

West leads the three of diamonds to his partner's queen. East returns the four of spades to the king and ace, and West continues with the ten of spades, East following with the three as you win with the queen. You elect to play West for the queen of hearts, cashing the ace and then finessing the jack. No luck! East produces the queen and returns the ace of diamonds. How do you cope with this development.

Review

The spades appear to be 4–2, but your contract will be in danger only if the clubs fail to run. Where do you ruff this diamond?

Solution

There is a temptation to discard a club from hand and ruff on the table. Then you could test the clubs, and you might be lucky enough to find that the defender with the club stopper also has the remaining trump.

But really, it would be an insult to your opponents to play like that. If the clubs were not running East would never have offered you a ruff and discard. He is not out to do you any favours, you may be sure.

The one thing you must not do is discard a club from hand on the ace of diamonds. You can either discard a spade from hand, ruff in dummy, draw the last trump and rely on the clubs, or you can ruff in hand, ruff a low spade with the heart king, draw the last trump, and cash your spades before playing on clubs.

The complete deal:

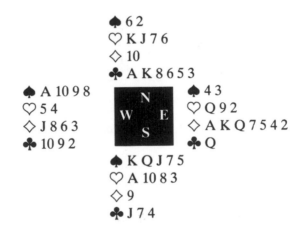

```
              ♠ 6 2
              ♡ K J 7 6
              ◇ 10
              ♣ A K 8 6 5 3
♠ A 10 9 8                    ♠ 4 3
♡ 5 4            N            ♡ Q 9 2
◇ J 8 6 3    W     E          ◇ A K Q 7 5 4 2
♣ 10 9 2        S            ♣ Q
              ♠ K Q J 7 5
              ♡ A 10 8 3
              ◇ 9
              ♣ J 7 4
```

PROBLEM 28

```
        ♠ A J 8 5
        ♡ 10 7
        ◇ K 6 3
        ♣ 7 5 4 3
                        N
                    W       E
                        S
                ♠ K Q 9 7 6
                ♡ 5 4
Game all.       ◇ A 10 7 4
Dealer East.    ♣ 9 6
```

The Bidding

WEST	NORTH	EAST	SOUTH
		1 ◇	Pass
1 ♠	Pass	2 ♡	Pass
3 ◇	Pass	3 NT	Pass
Pass	Pass		

The Lead

Your lead of the king of spades is won by the ace, East discarding the two of hearts. On the next play of the three of diamonds North discards the three of hearts and East plays the queen. How do you plan the defence?

Review

East's distribution must be 0–4–6–3, and there is no way of preventing him from scoring five diamond tricks. He has a spade trick already in the bag, and in view of his strong bidding he is likely to have three further winners – probably in hearts.

Solution

Obviously you cannot afford to give declarer a second spade trick, but if you hold up the ace of diamonds until the third round you will be able to cash the queen of spades. This may embarrass declarer if he cannot afford to part with a club.

But you can do better than that. To cause real anguish you should hold up the ace of diamonds until the fourth round, forcing declarer to use one of his heart entries. When you take the ace of diamonds and cash the queen of spades, the pressure may now be more than East can bear.

The complete deal:

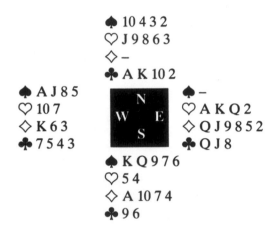

```
                    ♠ 10 4 3 2
                    ♡ J 9 8 6 3
                    ◇ -
                    ♣ A K 10 2
    ♠ A J 8 5           N           ♠ -
    ♡ 10 7          W       E       ♡ A K Q 2
    ◇ K 6 3             S           ◇ Q J 9 8 5 2
    ♣ 7 5 4 3                       ♣ Q J 8
                    ♠ K Q 9 7 6
                    ♡ 5 4
                    ◇ A 10 7 4
                    ♣ 9 6
```

North discards two spades and a club on the second, third and fourth diamonds, and your next play of the queen of spades forces East to part with a winning diamond. You return your second heart, of course, and partner is in a position to establish a heart as the setting trick.

PROBLEM 29

♠ K J 6 4
♡ A 5 4
◇ K Q J 4
♣ 7 2

♠ Q 5
♡ J 9 6
N–S game.   ◇ A 9 7 2
Dealer West.   ♣ K Q 8 6

The Bidding

WEST	NORTH	EAST	SOUTH
Pass	1 ◇	Dble	Rdble
1 ♡	Pass	Pass	3 ◇
Pass	3 ♡	Pass	3 NT
Pass	Pass	Pass	

The Lead

West leads the three of hearts to his partner's king. East returns the eight of hearts to the nine and ten, and West continues with the seven of hearts to knock out the ace, East following. When you play the four of spades from dummy East plays low and your queen wins the trick. How should you continue?

Review

You may hope to score one heart, four diamonds and two tricks in each of the black suits. The problem is to prevent East from taking five tricks first. Have you any ideas?

Solution

East is likely to have four cards in each black suit, and if you play a second spade at this point he will take his ace and continue the suit, establishing a fifth trick for the defence. The same thing will happen if you play clubs twice from dummy before establishing your second spade trick.

East will have only two diamonds, however, and he will come under pressure on the third round of the suit. Some heavy unblocking is needed. You should play the diamond seven to the jack, return a club to your queen, and continue with the diamond nine to dummy's queen. Now the play of the diamond king will force East to weaken his holding in one of the black suits.

The complete deal:

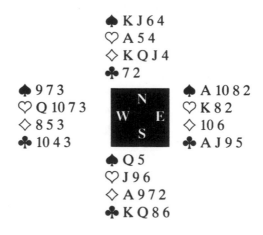

$\spadesuit$ K J 6 4
$\heartsuit$ A 5 4
$\diamondsuit$ K Q J 4
$\clubsuit$ 7 2

$\spadesuit$ 9 7 3
$\heartsuit$ Q 10 7 3
$\diamondsuit$ 8 5 3
$\clubsuit$ 10 4 3

$\spadesuit$ A 10 8 2
$\heartsuit$ K 8 2
$\diamondsuit$ 10 6
$\clubsuit$ A J 9 5

$\spadesuit$ Q 5
$\heartsuit$ J 9 6
$\diamondsuit$ A 9 7 2
$\clubsuit$ K Q 8 6

You have retained the option of winning the fourth round of diamonds in either hand, and East is caught in a seesaw squeeze. If he throws a club on the third diamond, you play the two from hand and continue with a club to establish two more tricks in the suit. If East throws a spade, you overtake with the ace of diamonds and play a spade to knock out the ace.

PROBLEM 30

♠ K Q J
♡ K J 9 7 3
◇ 8 4
♣ J 7 3

♠ 7 6 4 2
♡ 2
E–W game. ◇ A K Q 10 3
Dealer West. ♣ A K 5

The Bidding

WEST	NORTH	EAST	SOUTH
Pass	Pass	Pass	1 ◇
Pass	1 ♡	Pass	1 ♠
Pass	2 ♣	Pass	3 NT
Pass	Pass	Dble	Pass
Pass	Pass		

The Lead

West's lead of the eight of hearts is covered by the nine and ten. East returns the diamond seven to your ace. You play a spade and dummy's jack holds the trick. How should you continue?

Review

Clearly East has the high hearts sitting over dummy, and the ace of spades is marked in the West hand by East's initial pass. It does not look as though the diamonds are going to break, so you can count no more than seven top tricks.

Solution

An eighth trick may come from a 3–3 spade break, and the only chance of a ninth seems to lie in some sort of end-play against West. Before that can work you will have to cut communications between the defenders. West will presumably have no more than two hearts, and a high heart from dummy at this point will put the defenders out of touch with each other. You can discard a spade (or a diamond) from hand.

East cannot afford to cash a third heart while you still have a spade entry in dummy, so he will have to exit with a club or a diamond. Now you can knock out the ace of spades, win the spade return, and hope to throw West in with the fourth diamond to lead a club away from his queen.

The complete deal:

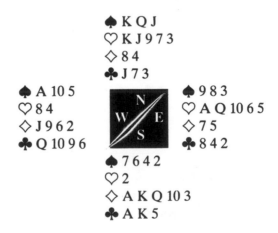

```
              ♠ K Q J
              ♡ K J 9 7 3
              ◇ 8 4
              ♣ J 7 3
 ♠ A 10 5                    ♠ 9 8 3
 ♡ 8 4          N            ♡ A Q 10 6 5
 ◇ J 9 6 2   W     E         ◇ 7 5
 ♣ Q 10 9 6     S            ♣ 8 4 2
              ♠ 7 6 4 2
              ♡ 2
              ◇ A K Q 10 3
              ♣ A K 5
```

East went astray when he switched to a diamond at trick two. If he had led a club you would have had no real chance.

[144]

PROBLEM 31

♠ A K Q 5
♡ 7 4 3
◇ A J 4
♣ 7 6 5

```
        N
    W       E
        S
```

♠ 7 6 2
♡ A 10
◇ 9 7 5 2
♣ A K Q 3

N–S game.
Dealer West.

The Bidding

WEST	NORTH	EAST	SOUTH
2 ♡*	Dble	Pass	3 ♡
Pass	3 ♠	Pass	3 NT
Pass	Pass	Pass	

Flannery, five hearts and four spades

The Lead

West attacks in hearts and you hold up your ace until the second round. Both defenders follow suit when you cash the ace of clubs. How should you continue?

Review

This is a reasonable contract although only eight tricks are in sight. West may well have done you a favour by deploying his pet convention, for you know that the spades are not breaking and you have a shrewd suspicion that the clubs will not break either.

Solution

West must surely have the king and queen of diamonds for his bid. He can therefore have no more than two clubs, and you may be able to squeeze him in diamonds and spades.

The first essential is to cut communications in hearts, so you should cross with a spade and play the third heart from the table. Either defender may win this trick, but no return can hurt you. If West wins and continues hearts, you can discard a club from dummy on the fourth round and a diamond on the fifth. When you cash your top clubs West will have to yield the ninth trick either in diamonds or in spades.

If West refuses to cash his long hearts, switching to a diamond or a spade, you simply play off the club winners. West is forced to abandon one of his heart winners, whereupon you can establish your ninth trick in diamonds.

The complete deal:

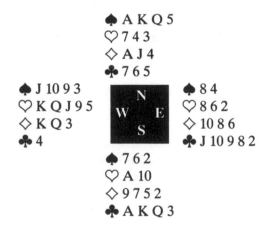

```
              ♠ A K Q 5
              ♡ 7 4 3
              ◇ A J 4
              ♣ 7 6 5
♠ J 10 9 3          N          ♠ 8 4
♡ K Q J 9 5    W       E       ♡ 8 6 2
◇ K Q 3            S          ◇ 10 8 6
♣ 4                           ♣ J 10 9 8 2
              ♠ 7 6 2
              ♡ A 10
              ◇ 9 7 5 2
              ♣ A K Q 3
```

Note that it would be fatal to play off the top clubs immediately. West would unblock in hearts, enabling East to win the third round and cash a couple of clubs. Dummy would be squeezed and the defenders would make five tricks.

You cannot afford even one more round of clubs before cutting communications in hearts.

PROBLEM 32

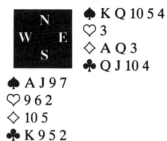

♠ K Q 10 5 4
♡ 3
♢ A Q 3
♣ Q J 10 4

♠ A J 9 7
♡ 9 6 2
♢ 10 5
♣ K 9 5 2

Love all.
Dealer West.

The Bidding

WEST	NORTH	EAST	SOUTH
Pass	Pass	1 ♠	Pass
2 ♡	Pass	2 ♠	Pass
2 NT	Pass	3 NT	Pass
Pass	Pass		

The Lead

North leads the seven of clubs to dummy's queen. How do you defend?

Review

Partner appears to have made a top-of-nothing lead, no doubt wishing to protect his honours in the red suits. That's all very well, but the club lead threatens an early demise for your king? Do you cover or duck?

Solution

If partner has three clubs, which is not unlikely, you can ensure a third-round trick for your king by withholding it on the first two rounds of the suit.

But there are wider considerations. You have to ask yourself where declarer proposes to go for his tricks. He may score three club tricks but he is unlikely to make more than two or three diamonds and one spade. The contract will have little chance unless declarer can develop several tricks in hearts.

The idea must be to attack the entries in the West hand before declarer can get the hearts going. You should therefore cover the queen of clubs with your king, even though this gives declarer an extra winner in clubs. The trick is likely to come back with interest in the later play.

The complete deal:

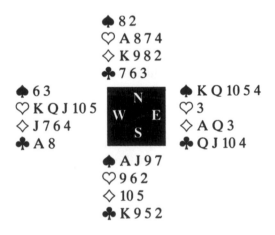

```
                    ♠ 8 2
                    ♡ A 8 7 4
                    ◇ K 9 8 2
                    ♣ 7 6 3
  ♠ 6 3                          ♠ K Q 10 5 4
  ♡ K Q J 10 5       N           ♡ 3
  ◇ J 7 6 4      W       E       ◇ A Q 3
  ♣ A 8              S           ♣ Q J 10 4
                    ♠ A J 9 7
                    ♡ 9 6 2
                    ◇ 10 5
                    ♣ K 9 5 2
```

Declarer has no real chance once his ace of clubs has been forced out. The best he can do is finesse the diamond queen, cash the top clubs and the diamond ace, and lead a heart to North's ace. North cashes the diamond king and leads a spade to the king and ace. After cashing your club you have to return a spade, but you still make a spade trick at the end.

PROBLEM 33

♠ K 7 6
♡ 9 7 3
◇ Q 5 2
♣ Q 6 3 2

♠ –
♡ A K Q J 6 5
◇ A K 7 6 4
♣ A 10

N–S game.
Dealer East.

The Bidding

WEST	NORTH	EAST	SOUTH
		2 ♠*	3 ♠
4 ♠	Pass	Pass	6 ♡
Pass	Pass	Pass	

*weak, 7–10

The Lead

West leads the queen of spades and dummy goes down with as much help as you have any right to expect. You play low from dummy and ruff in hand. You test the trumps with the ace and king, West following small and then discarding a spade. How should you continue?

Review

The 3–1 trump break will not matter if the diamonds break kindly, but West could have four cards in the suit. What can you do about it?

Solution

East is marked with the king of clubs as well as the ace of spades for his weak two bid. Consider what will happen if you leave the last trump at large and play on diamonds. If East has a singleton, he will not be able to ruff on the second or third rounds without end-playing himself in the black suits. But he will be able to over-ruff dummy on the fourth round and exit with the spade ace, since you have no further entry to dummy.

However, if West has the jack of clubs you may be able to end-play *him* on the fourth round of diamonds. You should cash the ace and king of diamonds at tricks four and five. If both defenders follow, you simply draw the last trump and claim your twelve tricks. If East discards on the second diamond, play a third diamond to the queen. East still cannot afford to ruff, and you make good use of this entry by ruffing a spade. Now concede a fourth diamond to West, discarding the king of spades from the table. With any luck West will have to concede your twelfth trick on the club return.

The complete deal:

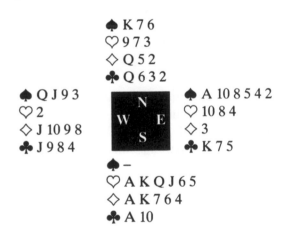

♠ K 7 6
♡ 9 7 3
♢ Q 5 2
♣ Q 6 3 2

♠ Q J 9 3
♡ 2
♢ J 10 9 8
♣ J 9 8 4

N
W E
S

♠ A 10 8 5 4 2
♡ 10 8 4
♢ 3
♣ K 7 5

♠ –
♡ A K Q J 6 5
♢ A K 7 6 4
♣ A 10

PROBLEM 34

♠ K 3
♡ J 9 5 2
♦ A 10 7 6 4
♣ K Q

```
    N
  W   E
    S
```

♠ Q J 10 4 2
♡ 8 6
♦ 3
♣ A 9 7 6 2

Love all.
Dealer East.

The Bidding

WEST	NORTH	EAST	SOUTH
		1 ♡	1 ♠
Pass	2 NT	Pass	3 ♣
Pass	3 ♠	Pass	Pass
Pass			

The Lead

West leads the seven of hearts to his partner's ten. East continues with the ace of hearts, West playing the four, and then the king of hearts. When you ruff with the two of spades West discards the three of clubs. How do you continue?

Review

The storm warnings are out. West's refusal to over-ruff makes it clear that he is nursing a four-card trump holding, and you are unlikely to succeed by straightforward play. Have you any ideas?

Solution

You are sure to lose control if you unblock the king and queen of clubs and continue with the king of spades from the table. If East has the ace he will scupper you with a further heart. If West has the spade ace he will hold up until the second round and then lead a diamond to lock you in dummy. You will be unable to reach your hand except by ruffing and the contract will go two down.

On this hand you must rely on a 3–3 club break and make full use of dummy's trumps. Play a club to the queen, overtake the king of clubs with your ace and continue with a third club. If West ruffs, you can safely over-ruff with the king and lead trumps. If West discards on the third club, you ruff in dummy with the three of spades, cash the ace of diamonds and cross-ruff for nine tricks.

The complete deal:

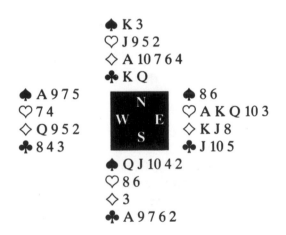

```
                    ♠ K 3
                    ♡ J 9 5 2
                    ◇ A 10 7 6 4
                    ♣ K Q
    ♠ A 9 7 5                      ♠ 8 6
    ♡ 7 4            N             ♡ A K Q 10 3
    ◇ Q 9 5 2    W      E          ◇ K J 8
    ♣ 8 4 3          S             ♣ J 10 5
                    ♠ Q J 10 4 2
                    ♡ 8 6
                    ◇ 3
                    ♣ A 9 7 6 2
```

PROBLEM 35

♠ K 6 4 3
♡ J 10
◇ 10 9
♣ K Q J 8 3

♠ 5
♡ A Q 9 8
◇ A K Q J 4
♣ 7 6 2

N–S game.
Dealer South.

The Bidding

SOUTH	WEST	NORTH	EAST
1 ◇	1 ♠	2 ♣	2 ♠
3 ♡	Pass	4 ◇	Pass
5 ◇	Pass	Pass	Pass

The Lead

West leads the nine of clubs. You play the king from dummy and East, after a momentary hesitation, follows with the five. On the third round of trumps West discards a spade. What do you throw from dummy on the third and fourth trumps, and how do you plan the play?

Review

East seems to have the club ace, in which case West is likely to have the ace of spades and the king of hearts. You appear to be in danger of losing three tricks.

Solution

It may be possible to succeed no matter who has the heart king. You must discard spades from dummy on the trumps, keeping the club length intact.

After drawing trumps play a second club to the queen. If the clubs are 3–2 East must hold off to kill the suit. (If he wins and returns a heart, you play the ace and dispose of your losing spade: if he wins and returns a spade, all your losing hearts will disappear on dummy's winners.) Now you turn your attention to West, leading the jack of hearts from dummy and covering with the queen.

What can West do if he has the king? If he wins and returns a heart, you take your three heart tricks and then lead a spade to establish your eleventh trick. If West cashes the spade ace before returning a heart, you win in dummy with the ten, discard your losing club on the spade king, and ruff yourself back to hand to enjoy two more hearts. Finally, if the queen of hearts wins (either because West holds up or because East has the king), you lead your spade and again eleven tricks must roll in one way or another.

The complete deal:

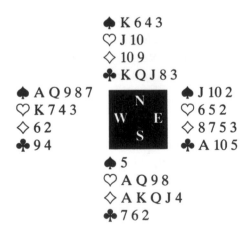

A spade lead and continuation would have defeated you by forcing you to make a premature discard on the spade king.

PROBLEM 36

♠ Q 10 3
♡ 8 4
◇ A K J 10 7 5 4
♣ 6

♠ 7 6
♡ A K 6 3
◇ Q 9 2
♣ A 7 4 2

Game all.
Dealer North.

The Bidding

WEST	NORTH	EAST	SOUTH
	Pass	1 ◇	Pass
1 ♠	Pass	2 ◇	Pass
3 ♣	Pass	3 ♠	Pass
4 ♠	Pass	Pass	Pass

The Lead

North leads the jack of hearts to your king. When you continue with the ace of hearts West drops the queen. What now?

Review

You can see three tricks for the defence. What about a fourth? It is not impossible for partner to have a trump trick, but if declarer's trumps are solid there is a danger that he will make his contract by setting up the diamonds.

Solution

The only way you might prevent the establishment of the diamonds is by forcing declarer to take a premature ruff in dummy. How might you force dummy? Not by cashing the ace of clubs and switching back to hearts, for declarer would take the ruff in hand and keep dummy's trumps intact.

Dummy can be forced only in clubs, and that requires partner to have a club honour. It will not do to play the ace and another club, for declarer might then be able to bring in the club suit, making ten tricks without bothering with the diamonds. You must switch to a low club at trick three, trusting that partner can win and return the suit.

The complete deal:

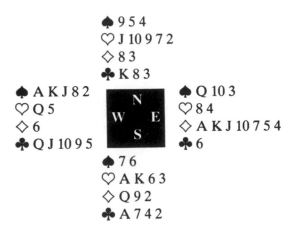

       ♠ 9 5 4
       ♡ J 10 9 7 2
       ♢ 8 3
       ♣ K 8 3

♠ A K J 8 2   ♠ Q 10 3
♡ Q 5   ♡ 8 4
♢ 6   ♢ A K J 10 7 5 4
♣ Q J 10 9 5   ♣ 6

       ♠ 7 6
       ♡ A K 6 3
       ♢ Q 9 2
       ♣ A 7 4 2

The defence of a low club at trick three is sure to win if partner has the king of clubs and a trump as high as the eight, and it may even succeed when he has the club queen. If partner has nothing in clubs, you will still prevail if he has a trump trick.